Cambridge English for
Engineering

Mark Ibbotson

Series Editor: Jeremy Day

CAMBRIDGE
UNIVERSITY PRESS

University Printing House, Cambridge CB2 8BS, United Kingdom

Cambridge University Press is part of the University of Cambridge.

It furthers the University's mission by disseminating knowledge in the pursuit of education, learning and research at the highest international levels of excellence

www.cambridge.org
Information on this title: www.cambridge.org/9780521715188

First published 2008
13th printing 2015

Printed in Italy by Rotolito Lombarda S.p.A.

A catalogue record for this publication is available from the British Library

ISBN 978-0-521-71518-8 Student's Book with Audio CDs (2)

Introduction

The aim of *Cambridge English for Engineering* is to improve your professional communication skills, whether you are an engineer, an engineering technician or a technical manager. The course covers high-priority language that is useful in any branch of engineering (mechanical, electrical, civil, etc.), focusing on skills such as working with drawings, describing technical problems and discussing dimensions and precision. Each of the ten units contains:

- realistic listening activities so you can learn the language used in technical discussions
- situation-based speaking activities so you can practise the language you've learned
- relevant vocabulary presented and practised in professional contexts
- engaging topics and articles to make your learning interesting and motivating.

On the audio you will hear people in the kinds of situation often encountered at work, for example safety meetings, project briefings and problem-solving discussions. Audioscripts for the listening exercises and a complete answer key, including suggested answers for the discussion activities, are at the back of the book.

You can also find engineering case studies and extra activities online at www.cambridge.org/elt/englishforengineering.

How to use *Cambridge English for Engineering* for self-study

If you are working on your own, you can do the units in any order you like. Choose the topic that you want to look at and work through the unit, doing the exercises and checking your answers in the answer key. Note any mistakes you make, and go back and listen or read again to help you understand what the problem was. For the listening exercises, it's better to listen more than once and to look at the audioscript after the exercise so that you can read the language you've just heard. For the speaking activities, *think* about what you would say in the situation. You could also try talking about the discussion points with your colleagues.

I hope you enjoy using the course. If you have any comments on *Cambridge English for Engineering* you can email me at englishforengineering@cambridge.org

Mark Ibbotson

Mark Ibbotson has a BSc (Hons) degree in Construction management, and a BTEC National Diploma in Civil Engineering. He spent the initial years of his career in site engineering and technical management positions on construction projects in the UK. Since relocating to France and entering the field of in-company language training, he has designed and taught technical English courses in a wide range of companies, for process, mechanical, electrical, civil and highway engineers, as well as technicians and technical managers. Mark is the author of *Professional English in Use Engineering* (Cambridge University Press) and also co-author of the *Business Start-Up* series (Cambridge University Press).

- Describing technical functions and applications
- Explaining how technology works
- Emphasising technical advantages
- Simplifying and illustrating technical explanations

Describing technical functions and applications

1 a In pairs, think about two or three products you use regularly and discuss the following questions.

- What are the main functions of the products? (What do they do?)
- What are their different applications? (What are they used for?)

b What do you know about Global Positioning System (GPS) devices? In pairs, describe their main function, and give some examples of different applications of GPS devices.

2 a ▶1.1 Paula, a design engineer for a GPS manufacturer, is discussing product development with José, a senior manager new to the company. Listen to the conversation and complete the following notes.

- the primary application of GPS   (1) _____
- associated applications   Tracking systems for (2) _____
  Tracking systems for (3) _____
- more creative features   (4) _____/alarms
  (5) _____ buttons
- not technical innovations   (6) _____ the technology

b Complete the following extracts from the discussion with words that come from *use*.

1 *Then you've got associated applications, _____ that are related to navigating …*
2 *… tracking systems you can _____ for monitoring delivery vehicles …*
3 *… from the end-_____ point of view, accuracy is no longer the main selling point. Most devices are accurate enough. The key is to make them more _____ .*

3 **a** Match the GPS applications (1–6) to the descriptions (a–f).

1	topographical surveying	a	navigation and safety at sea
✓ 2	geological exploration	b	setting out positions and levels of new structures
✓ 3	civil engineering	c	mapping surface features
✓ 4	avionics equipment	d	applications in mining and the oil industry
✓ 5	maritime applications	e	highway navigation and vehicle tracking
✓ 6	GPS in cars and trucks	f	air traffic control, navigation and autopilot systems

b In pairs, practise explaining the applications of GPS in Exercise 3a to a colleague who has limited knowledge of the devices using the following phrases.

> used for -ing   used to   useful for   another / a similar use

4 **a** Complete the following extracts from the conversation by underlining the correct words.

1 ... there's a setting on the GPS that **allows**/**prevents** it to detect the movement ...

2 ... an alarm sounds to warn you, and **allows**/**prevents** the boat from drifting unnoticed.

3 ... and **enables**/**ensures** that you don't lose track of where you were, which then **enables**/**ensures** you to turn round and come back to the same point ...

b Match the words in Exercise 4a to the synonyms.

1 _____ = makes sure   2 _____ / _____ = permits   3 _____ = stops

c Complete the following extract from the user's manual of a GPS device using the verbs in Exercise 4a. Sometimes, more than one answer is possible.

> ┌─ INTRODUCTION ──────────────────────
> The core function of your GPS receiver is to (1) _____ you to locate your precise
> geographical position. To (2) _____ the device to function, it receives at least three
> signals simultaneously from the GPS constellation – 30 dedicated satellites which
> (3) _____ receivers can function anywhere on earth. To (4) _____ extremely precise
> positioning and (5) _____ errors from occurring due to external factors, this device is
> designed to receive four separate signals (see enhanced system accuracy on page 18).

(handwritten annotations: enable, allow, enable, 4 = allow)

5 In pairs, explain the main functions and applications of a product made by your company or a product you know about. Student A, you are an engineering manager; Student B, you are a new employee. Use the language from this section and the phrases in the box. Swap roles and practise again.

> I see. So ...   OK. In other words ...   So you mean ...

Explaining how technology works

6 a **In pairs, look at the picture and discuss the following questions.**

- How do you think a space elevator would work?
- What could it be used for?
- What technical challenges would it face?
- How seriously do you think the concept of space elevators is being taken at present?

b **Read the following article and compare it to your answers in Exercise 6a.**

Space elevators: preparing for takeoff

IN his 1979 novel, *The Fountains of Paradise*, Arthur C Clarke wrote about an elevator **connecting** the earth's surface to space. Three decades later, this science-fiction concept is preparing to take off in the real world. NASA has launched the Space Elevator Challenge, a competition with a generous prize fund, and several teams and companies are working on serious research projects aimed at winning it.

As its name suggests, a space elevator is designed to **raise** things into space. Satellites, components for space ships, supplies for astronauts in space stations, and even astronauts themselves are examples of payloads that could be **transported** into orbit without the need

for explosive and environmentally unfriendly rockets. However, the altitude of orbital space – a colossal 35,790 km above the earth – is a measure of the challenge facing engineers. How could such a height be reached?

The answer is by using an incredibly strong and lightweight cable, strong enough to **support** its own weight and a heavy load. The design of such a cable is still largely theoretical. This would be **attached** to a base station on earth at one end and a satellite in geostationary orbit (fixed above a point on the equator) at the other. Lift vehicles would then **ascend** and **descend** the cable, **powered** by electromagnetic force and **controlled** remotely.

c **Match the verbs (1–9) from the text in Exercise 6b to the definitions (a–i).**

e	1	connecting	a	carried (objects, over a distance)
i	2	raise	b	hold something firmly / bear its weight
a	3	transported	c	climb down
b	4	support	d	provided with energy / moved by a force
g	5	attached	e	joining
h	6	ascend	f	driven / have movement directed
c	7	descend	g	fixed
d	8	powered	h	climb up
f	9	controlled	i	lift / make something go up

7 a **James, an engineer, is giving a talk on space elevators. Complete his notes using the correct form of the verbs (1–9) in Exercise 6c.**

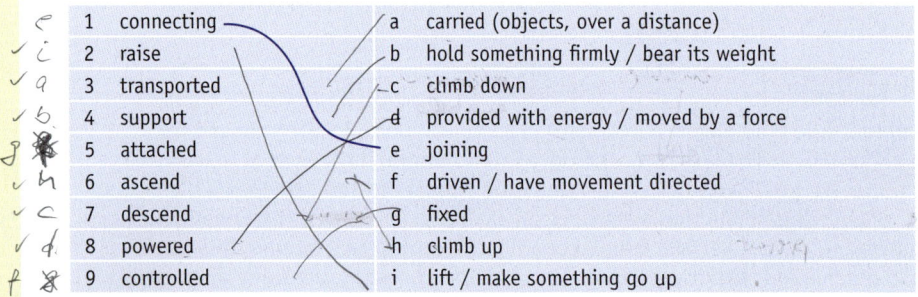

Space Elevators

- *Challenge of (1) __connecting__ a satellite to earth by cable is significant.*
- *To (2) _____ its own weight, and be securely (3) _____ at each end, cable would need phenomenal strength-to-weight ratio.*
- *How could vehicles be (4) _____ into space, up cable?*
- *Self-contained energy source problematic, due to weight (heavy fuel or batteries required to (5) _____ vehicle).*
- *Two possible ways round problem:*
  1 Transmit electricity wirelessly. But technique only at research stage.
  2 Solar power. But would only allow vehicle to (6) _____ slowly. Not necessarily a problem, as car could be controlled remotely, allowing it to (7) _____ payloads unmanned.

b ▶1.2 Listen to part of James' talk and check your answers in Exercise 7a.

c What kinds of word are missing from the notes? In pairs, compare the audioscript on page 86 with the notes in Exercise 7a.

8 a Some space elevator designs propose an offshore base station. In pairs, discuss how such a system might work using words in Exercise 6c. What advantages might an offshore base have compared with a land base?

b ▶1.3 James goes on to discuss offshore base stations. Listen to the talk and answer the following questions.

1 How would an offshore base station be supported?
2 What would the function of its anchors be?
3 How would payloads reach the base station?
4 What problem would a mobile base station help to prevent?
5 What would the procedure be if there was an alert?

Payload = loading   seafloor ⎱ means-
*   sea bed ⎰ ground*

9 a You are members of a space elevator research team designing a concept for offshore base stations. In pairs, analyse the notes below, which were made during a briefing given by your manager. Imagine you are giving a presentation. Begin by reading out the abbreviated notes in full.

OFFSHORE BASE STATION - ANCHORING & PROPULSION ISSUES

Anchoring system

Wind loads on cable will be huge. What implications for anchoring system?
Base will need to be moved continually, sometimes urgently. What temp system could be used to hold base in position?
Base in shallow water near coast, or deep water further offshore? Choice will have impact on design of anchor system.

Propulsion system

Will weight of cable allow base to be moved by own propellers? Or more powerful system for propulsion and control nec.? E.g. extern. power source?

b In pairs, discuss the questions raised in the notes and think of some suitable solutions for the anchoring system and the propulsion system. At this stage, these should be overall concepts, not detailed designs. Remember to make notes.

c In small groups, take turns to give a short talk using your notes to explain how the systems work, in general terms. Imagine you are speaking to a small group of colleagues, including your manager.

d Write two or three paragraphs to summarise your talk. These will be included in your manager's longer report on offshore base stations.

Emphasising technical advantages

10 In pairs, discuss the term *technical advantage*. Give some examples of technology you are familiar with.

11 **a** Read the first paragraph of some promotional literature from Otis, a leading elevator company. What is the Gen2™ system?

b Match the words (1–6) from the text in Exercise 11a to the synonyms (a–f).

1	conventional	a	decreases
2	eliminates	b	better / the best
3	superior	c	improved
4	energy-efficient	d	standard, usual
5	enhanced	e	gets rid of
6	reduces	f	has low energy consumption

c Complete the following text using the correct form of the words (1–6) in Exercise 11b. You will need to use some words more than once.

OTIS Unique Flat Belt

The key to Otis's patented drive technology

At the heart of the Gen2™ elevator system is a flat belt (developed by and unique to Otis). It is just 3mm thick. Yet it is stronger than **conventional** steel cables. It lasts up to three times longer. And it has enabled Otis to completely re-invent the elevator. The flat, coated-steel belt totally **eliminates** the metal-to-metal effect of conventional systems. Coupled with a smooth-surface crowned machine sheave, the result is exceptionally quiet operation and **superior** ride comfort. Furthermore, the flexible flat belt enables a more compact, **energy-efficient** machine, which can be contained in the hoistway. This **enhanced** technology **reduces** building and system operating costs, and frees up valuable space.

Protecting the environment

Neither the belt nor the gearless machine, with its permanently sealed bearings, requires any lubrication so the Gen2™ system is cleaner for the environment. The highly (1) _energy-efficient_ gearless machine, with its permanent-magnet synchronous motor, (2) _____ power consumption by as much as 50 percent over (3) _____ geared machines and 15 percent over other machines with permanent-magnet motors of axial construction.

Reliable by design

Long-lasting flat belts, smooth, crowned sheaves and minimal moving parts in the gearless machine dramatically (4) _____ wear and increase durability and efficiency. To further (5) _____ reliability and safety, Otis developed the Pulse™ system, which continually monitors the status of the belts' steel cords. Unlike visual inspections of (6) _____ steel ropes, the Pulse™ system automatically detects and reports belt faults to maintenance personnel for rapid response, providing owners with greater peace of mind. With flat belt technology, Otis has created a (7) _____ system that (8) _____ the need for a machine room, is quiet, clean, reliable and economical, and easy to install and maintain.

d In pairs, summarise the advantages of the flat belt system. Discuss durability, wear, noise, space, cleanliness, efficiency, automation, maintenance and cost.

12 a Complete the following tips on emphasising technical advantages using the words in the box.

conventional   eliminated   enhanced   reduced   superior

When describing technical advantages, it's useful to emphasise …
a   (1) _____ performance, compared with the older model of the same product.
b   negative issues that have been (2) _____ , or completely (3) _____ .
c   special features that differentiate the technology from (4) _____ systems.
d   performance levels that make the technology (5) _____ to the competition.

b ▶1.4 **Stefan, an engineer, is briefing some sales colleagues on the advantages of a new pump design. Listen to the briefing and match the tips (a–d) in Exercise 12a to the extracts (1–4).**

Extract 1 _____   Extract 2 _____   Extract 3 _____   Extract 4 _____

c Complete the following sentences from the briefing by underlining the correct emphasising word.
1   *We've come up with a **completely**/**significantly** unique profile.*
2   *It **completely**/**dramatically** reduces vibration.*
3   *Machines like these can never be **entirely**/**highly** free from vibration.*
4   *The new design runs **dramatically**/**extremely** smoothly.*
5   *Another advantage of the new profile is that it's **considerably**/**entirely** lighter.*
6   *So compared with our previous range, it's **highly**/**totally** efficient.*
7   *Trials so far suggest the design is **completely**/**exceptionally** durable.*
8   *We expect it to be **entirely**/**significantly** more reliable than rival units.*

d Match the words in Exercise 12c to the synonyms.

considerably   dramatically   entirely   exceptionally   highly   totally

1   _____ / _____ = completely
2   _____ / _____ = significantly
3   _____ / _____ = extremely

13 You are Otis engineers back in the 1850s, when elevators were new. In pairs, prepare a short talk to brief your sales colleagues on the advantages of elevators for lifting people and goods. Emphasise the points below, using the phrases and techniques from this section. Remember that people at this time are sceptical about the technology.

Elevators are …
●   safe – a reliable braking system eliminates the danger of a car falling if a cable fails
●   simple – they're controlled from the car and are very easy to operate
●   convenient – they're easier on the legs than the conventional alternative (stairs)
●   valuable – they enhance the value of land by allowing taller buildings on smaller areas

Simplifying and illustrating technical explanations

14 **a** ▶1.5 Richard, a structural engineer, often takes clients on guided tours of their new buildings during construction. He is talking about explaining technical concepts to non-specialists. Listen and answer the following questions.

1   What does Richard say about explaining technical concepts?
2   What does he mean by *dull* explanations?
3   What is *being patronising*?

b In pairs, think of some tips on how to solve the following problems.

1   not being understood
2   being patronising
3   explaining difficult concepts
4   sounding dull

c ▶1.6 Richard is giving some advice about the problems in Exercise 14b. Listen and summarise his ideas. Compare his tips with your suggestions.

15 **a** Richard has made notes for a guided tour of a site. The project is a skyscraper in the early stages of construction. During the tour he explains the technical terms to the non-specialist group. In pairs, discuss the following terms and try to interpret them using everyday language to rephrase them.

SUBSTRUCTURE

- *Pile foundations (in general)*
- *Bored in situ concrete piles*
- *Pre-cast driven concrete piles*
- *Pile driver*
- *Pile auger*
- *Bentonite*

Pile = Haufen / Stapel
auger = Bohrer / Förderschnecke

b ▶1.7 Richard is giving a tour of a construction site. Listen and make notes of his explanations of the following technical terms. Compare your ideas with his.

1   the substructure the part of the structure below ground
2   a pile foundation ....
3   to bore (a pile) ....
4   in situ concrete ....
5   pre-cast piles ....
6   to drive in (a pile) ....
7   a pile driver ....
8   a pile auger ....
9   bentonite ....

c ▶1.7 Listen again and compare Richard's explanations with the tips in Exercise 14c. Which techniques did he use? Were they successful?

d Complete the following table using the words in the box.

basically (x2) call effectively essentially imagine other
picture refer ~~simple~~ simply

Function	Words / Phrases
1 Simplifying the language	in _simple_ terms / put _____ / in _____ words / _____
2 Simplifying the concept	_____ / _____ / _____
3 Focusing on technical terms	what we _____ / what we _____ to as
4 Illustrating with images	if you _____ / if you _____

e In pairs, practise explaining the technical terms in Exercise 15a using the simplified words and phrases in Exercise 15d.

16 Read the textbook description of two types of pile foundation. Use the words and phrases in Exercise 15d and the following notes to rephrase it.

From a structural perspective, pile foundations can be divided into two categories: end-bearing piles and friction piles.

End-bearing piles are driven or bored through soft ground in order to attain firm substrata below. The pile then transmits load vertically to firm subsoil or bedrock. The soft ground surrounding the sides of the pile is structurally redundant.

Imagine water and the seabed

Like standing on stilts in water

Friction piles counteract downward loads from the structure through frictional resistance between the sides of the pile and the surrounding ground, and do not therefore rely on firm substrata. In some cases, the diameter of the concrete at the pile's base is widened by compaction, allowing the increased area to give the friction pile a certain degree of end-bearing resistance.

Like a nail in wood

Imagine a leg and a foot

17 You are showing a non-specialist visitor around your company and explaining technical concepts using simplified language. In pairs, practise explaining a product or type of technology that you are familiar with.

UNIT 2 Materials technology

- Describing specific materials
- Categorising materials
- Specifying and describing properties
- Discussing quality issues

Describing specific materials

1 **In pairs, discuss the benefits and problems of recycling. Use the following examples and your own ideas.**

breaking up ships   demolishing buildings   recycling electronics   scrapping cars

2 a **Read the following web page and complete the missing headings using the words in the box.**

Aluminium   Copper   Glass   Plastic   Rubber   ~~Steel~~   Timber

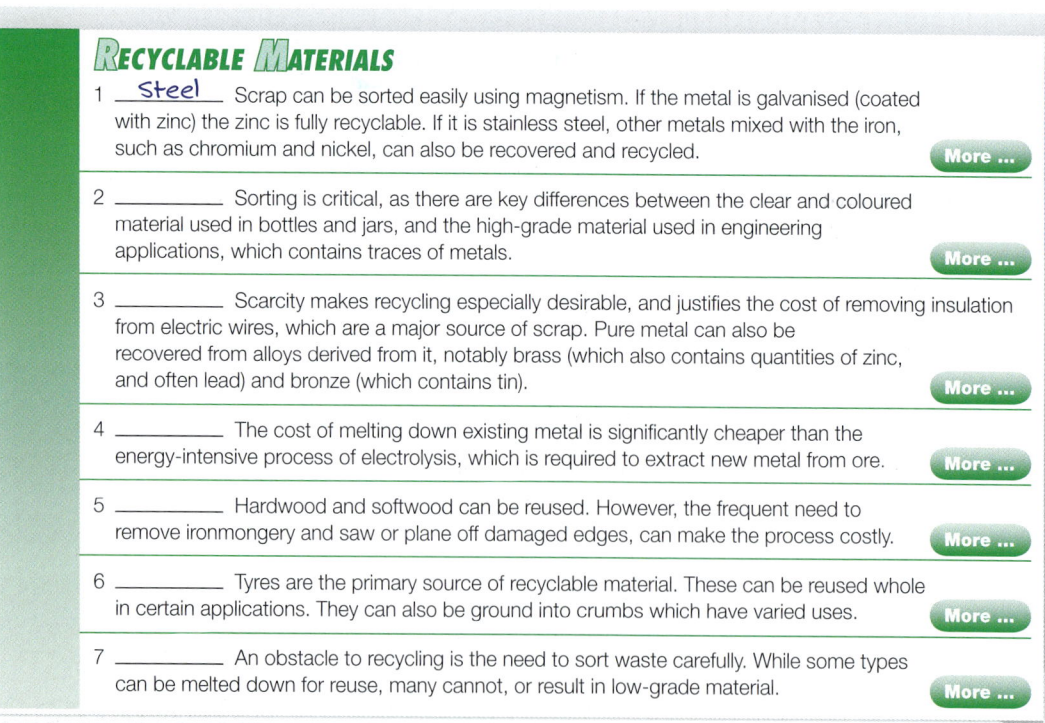

RECYCLABLE MATERIALS

1 __Steel__ Scrap can be sorted easily using magnetism. If the metal is galvanised (coated with zinc) the zinc is fully recyclable. If it is stainless steel, other metals mixed with the iron, such as chromium and nickel, can also be recovered and recycled.   More ...

2 _____ Sorting is critical, as there are key differences between the clear and coloured material used in bottles and jars, and the high-grade material used in engineering applications, which contains traces of metals.   More ...

3 _____ Scarcity makes recycling especially desirable, and justifies the cost of removing insulation from electric wires, which are a major source of scrap. Pure metal can also be recovered from alloys derived from it, notably brass (which also contains quantities of zinc, and often lead) and bronze (which contains tin).   More ...

4 _____ The cost of melting down existing metal is significantly cheaper than the energy-intensive process of electrolysis, which is required to extract new metal from ore.   More ...

5 _____ Hardwood and softwood can be reused. However, the frequent need to remove ironmongery and saw or plane off damaged edges, can make the process costly.   More ...

6 _____ Tyres are the primary source of recyclable material. These can be reused whole in certain applications. They can also be ground into crumbs which have varied uses.   More ...

7 _____ An obstacle to recycling is the need to sort waste carefully. While some types can be melted down for reuse, many cannot, or result in low-grade material.   More ...

b Match the materials from the web page (1–8) in Exercise 2 to the definitions (a–h).

1	stainless steel	a	a metal used to make brass, and in galvanised coatings on steel
2	zinc	b	the predominant metal in steel
3	iron	c	a type of steel not needing a protective coating, as it doesn't rust
4	bronze	d	a dense, poisonous metal
5	lead	e	rocks from which metals can be extracted
6	hardwood	f	an alloy made from copper and tin
7	ore	g	timber from pine trees
8	softwood	h	timber from deciduous trees

c Complete the following sentences using *from*, *with* or *of*.

1 Bronze contains significant amounts __of__ copper.
2 Galvanised steel is steel coated _____ zinc.
3 Steel is an alloy derived _____ iron.
4 Pure metals can usually be recovered _____ alloys.
5 To produce stainless steel, iron is mixed _____ other metals.
6 Stainless steel contains quantities _____ chromium and nickel.
7 Glass tableware contains traces _____ metals, such as lead.
8 When new metal is extracted _____ ore, the costs can be high.

d In pairs, ask and answer questions about different materials using the following phrases.

Can ... be recycled?   What's ... made from?   Where does ... come from?

3 a Irina, an ecological adviser, is talking to a group of engineers on a training course about environmentally friendly design. In pairs, discuss the ideas from her slide and give some examples.

Environmental audit

Product phases:
- Pre-use
- In use
- Post-use

b ▶2.1 Listen to an extract from the talk and compare your ideas with what Irina says. What example does she use to illustrate her main point?

c ▶2.2 Irina asks the engineers to do a simplified environmental audit. Their task is to compare steel and aluminium car bodywork from an ecological perspective. Listen to Sophia and Pete, two of the engineers, discussing the topic and make notes of their ideas.

d In pairs, do an environmental audit for the following applications and materials. Use the words and phrases in the box.

	Application	Materials
1	electrical wires in vehicles	copper and aluminium
2	external walls in houses	bricks and softwood

as far as I know ...   I think so / I'd say so   I'm (not) sure
that's an important consideration   that needs to be researched
coated   derived   mixed   recovered   recycled

Categorising materials

4 **What do you know about braking systems? In pairs, discuss the following questions.**

1 Generally speaking, what do brakes do and how do they work?
2 What kinds of material are used in brake pads and brake discs in different vehicles?

5 **a** **Read the article on braking systems. In the title of the article, what do the colours green and red refer to?**

b **In pairs, answer the following questions.**

1 Why do most braking systems waste energy?
2 What are regenerative braking systems, and how do they save energy?
3 What characteristics are required of materials used for the brakes on racing cars?
4 What is meant by *heat soak*, and why is it a problem in racing cars?

GREEN BRAKES
– A RED HOT TOPIC IN MOTOR RACING

As motor racing goes green, Formula 1 is aiming to lead automotive research in finding hi-tech efficiency gains. One of the keys to this ecological drive is regenerative braking (also known as kinetic energy recovery), which recovers energy generated during deceleration, and stores it as a source of power for subsequent acceleration.

Regenerative brakes limit the energy loss inherent in traditional braking systems. In most vehicles, conventional brakes comprise pads previously made from asbestos-based composites, but now consisting of **compounds*** of **exotic**, non-hazardous

materials, and discs made of **ferrous** metal. The resulting friction generates heat, which is wasted. In performance cars, this phenomenon is taken to extremes, and due to the high temperatures generated, brake discs are often made out of **ceramics**.

The carbon discs and pads used on Formula 1 cars generate so much heat that they glow red hot. High temperatures are, in fact, necessary for the effective operation of carbon brakes. But there's still plenty of potential for recovering the kinetic energy, rather than merely dissipating it in the form of heat.

The potential for recovering energy also extends to the heat generated by engines and exhaust systems. This area has also been discussed as a possible area for future exploitation in motor racing. Heat recovery might offer the added benefit of reducing heat soak (thermal absorption by the chassis) as delicate **alloy** parts and sensitive **non-metallic** materials, such as **polymers**, are susceptible to heat damage.

c **Match the materials from the text (1–7) to the descriptions (a–g).**

1	compounds	a	materials that are not metal
2	exotic	b	iron and steel
3	ferrous	c	combinations of materials
4	ceramics	d	mixture of metals
5	alloy	e	plastic materials
6	non-metallic	f	minerals transformed by heat
7	polymers	g	rare or complex

d In pairs, take turns to describe an object using the words from Exercise 5c and the phrases in the box. Ask your partner to guess what it is.

> comprise   consist of   made from   made of   made out of

6 **a** You are going to give a talk on composites technology at a construction materials trade fair. In part of the talk, you focus on reinforced concrete as a well-known example of a composite material. Prepare your talk using words and phrases from this section and the following notes.

> ## Composite materials
>
> Common example: reinforced concrete (very widely used composite)
>
> Cement (derived from lime)
>
> Aggregate – fine aggregate (sand) + coarse aggregate (gravel or crushed stone)
>
> Water + chemical additives (e.g. plasticiser to improve workability)
>
> Reinforcement (steel bars, fixed together with steel tie wire)

b In small groups, take turns to give your talk.

c Margit, a sales engineer, is describing a high-voltage cable. Before you listen, label the cross-section with the parts (a–e).

  a insulation
  b waterproof membrane
  c outer jacket
  d armoured protection
  e conductor

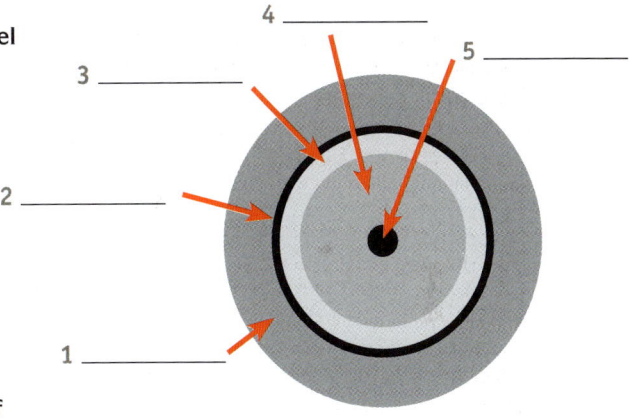

3 _____
4 _____
5 _____
2 _____
1 _____

d ▶2.3 Listen to the description and check your answers in Exercise 6c.

e Match the parts of the cable (a–e) in Exercise 6c to the following categories of materials (1–5). You will need to use some parts more than once.

1 non-metallic _a_ _____ _____
2 metallic _____ _____
3 ferrous metal _____
4 non-ferrous metal _____
5 polymer-based _____ _____ _____

7 Imagine you are presenting a product or appliance you know well to a potential client. Describe the categories of material used to make the different parts.

Specifying and describing properties

8 **a** In pairs, discuss what you know about the properties of Kevlar® and how it is used.

b Read the following extract from DuPont™'s technical guide to Kevlar®. Compare the information with your ideas from Exercise 8a.

WHAT IS KEVLAR®?

DuPont™ KEVLAR® is an organic fiber in the aromatic polyamide family. The unique properties and distinct chemical composition of KEVLAR® distinguish it from other commercial, man-made fibers.

KEVLAR® has a unique combination of high modulus, toughness, abrasion resistance and thermal stability. It was developed for demanding industrial and advanced-technology applications. Currently, many types of KEVLAR® are produced to meet a broad range of end uses that require strong, lightweight, durable materials.

Copyright DuPont de Nemours

DuPont™ and Kevlar® are registered trademarks or trademarks of E.I.du Pont de Nemours Company or its affiliates

c Find words in the text in Exercise 8b to match the following definitions.

1 _toughness_ = the opposite of fragility
2 _____ = resistance to damage caused by friction
3 _____ = resistance to problems caused by temperature change
4 _____ = long-lasting
5 _____ = the opposite of heavy

9 **a** Match the automotive parts (1–5) to the descriptions (a–e).

1	drive belts	a	sheets inserted between parts to prevent gas or fluid leakage
2	brake pads	b	pneumatic envelopes in contact with the road surface
3	tyres	c	flexible bands used in transmission systems
4	sealing gaskets	d	protective barriers capable of resisting gunshots
5	bullet-resistant armour	e	pads pressed against discs to induce deceleration

b Read the information from DuPont™ on the following page explaining some of the automotive applications of Kevlar®. Complete the text using the automotive parts in Exercise 9a.

Car and truck (1) _____ have incorporated Kevlar® into their construction because it offers superb puncture, abrasion and tear resistance.

The high modulus and abrasion resistance of Kevlar® help (2) _____ retain their original shape and tension over the millions of revolutions they go through over the lifespan of a vehicle.

The frictional forces that (3) _____ are designed to endure take less of a toll on those made with Kevlar® pulp. The enhanced thermal stability and inherent abrasion resistance of Kevlar®

allow them to last long and stop the vehicle safely and quietly.

Kevlar® provides an effective, lightweight (4) _____ solution for vehicles that require protection against ballistic attack, allowing cars and light trucks to retain most of their original handling characteristics.

Chemical stability and thermal stability help make (5) _____ reinforced with Kevlar® pulp strong and durable. The galvanic corrosion resistance of Kevlar® also contributes to improved long-term engine performance.

C In pairs, discuss why the properties of Kevlar® are especially important for each application described in the text.

10 a ▶2.4 Listen to a conversation about the properties of materials used in a specific type of tool and answer the following questions.

1 Where does the conversation take place?
2 What tool is being discussed?
3 Which materials can be used for its different parts?

b ▶2.4 Complete the following extracts from the conversation using the properties in Exercise 8c. Listen again and check your answers.

1 The handle mustn't be heavy. *Ideally, you want it to be _____ .*
2 Resisting friction is essential. *The key requirement is _____ _____ .*
3 The bur has to be built to last. *Obviously, they need to be very _____ .*
4 Heat builds up in the bur. *You need a good degree of _____ _____ .*

c Match the words and phrases (1–5) from Exercise 10b to the synonyms (a–e).

1	ideally	a	it's clear that
2	obviously	b	for the best results
3	the last thing you want	c	the most important factor
4	the key requirement	d	a lot of / a high level of
5	a good degree of	e	the worst situation

11 a You work for a manufacturer of hand tools and have been asked to investigate using alternative materials in your products. In pairs, read the notes and discuss the main properties required of the materials used to make the tools.

Hammers   a) Joiners' hammers (for nails)
                   b) Lump hammers (for masonry chisels)
Consider the hammer head and the hammer shaft.

Saws   a) Wood saws (for cutting wood)
                   b) Hacksaws (for cutting metal)
Consider the saw blade and the saw handle or frame.

b Think of a product you know well.
In pairs, discuss the materials used in it and what properties make the materials suitable. Discuss whether alternative materials could be used.

Discussing quality issues

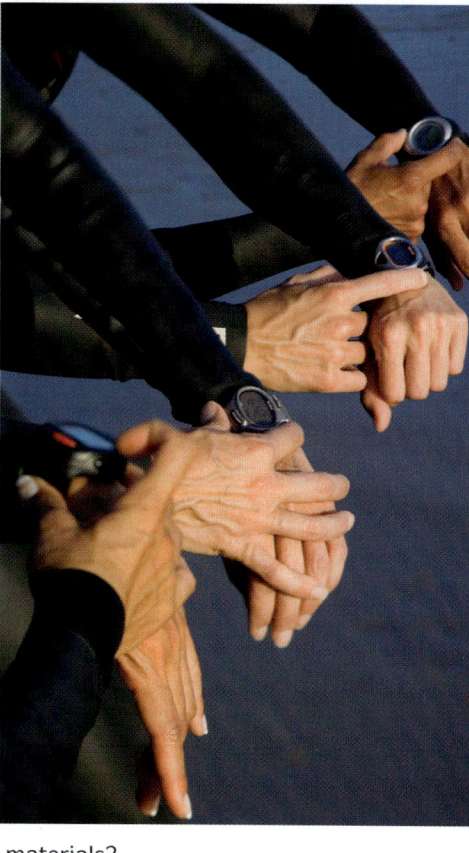

12 **In pairs, answer the following questions.**

1 In advertising, what hi-tech, high-performance situations are often used to promote watches?
2 What messages are they intended to send about the quality of products?
3 What quality issues differentiate higher-quality watches from lower-quality ones?
4 What is the difference between describing something as water-resistant and waterproof?

13 **a** ▶ 2.5 **Louisa, a marketing executive for a watch manufacturer, is discussing material selection with Tom, one of her engineering colleagues. Listen to the discussion and complete the four quality issues that are mentioned in the meeting.**

1 _____ resistance
2 _____ resistance
3 _____ resistance
4 _____ resistance

b **In pairs, discuss what is meant by each of the quality issues in Exercise 13a.**

14 **a** ▶ 2.5 **Listen again and answer the following questions.**

1 What point does Tom make about the reasons for selecting materials?
2 What does he say about submarine-grade steel to exemplify the above point?
3 What problem does he describe with regard to the marketability of many materials?
4 What hard commercial fact does Louisa give?

b **In pairs, mark the following statements True (T) or False (F) according to the views expressed in the conversation. Read the audioscript on page 87 and check your answers.**

1 Often, exotic-sounding materials are not that suitable, technically.
2 People think that a submarine steel watch must be tremendously water-resistant.
3 The corrosion resistance of submarine steel is exceptionally good.
4 Submarine-grade steel looks fairly good.
5 Tom thinks submarine steel is particularly suitable for watches.
6 The firm has often used materials that are not adequately durable.
7 Often, the compositions of good watch materials are relatively complex.
8 Materials with complicated names are pretty good for marketing.

c ▶2.6 **Listen to the following phrases from the conversation and underline the stressed syllable. Practise saying the phrases.**

1 not par<u>tic</u>ularly suitable
2 exceptionally resistant
3 not at all suitable
4 tremendously marketable
5 relatively complex
6 not all that good

d **Complete the following table using the words in the box.**

| exceptionally | fairly | insufficiently | not adequately | not (all) that |
| not particularly | pretty | relatively | tremendously | not at all |

extremely	quite	not very	not enough	definitely not
exceptionally				

15 **In pairs, discuss the key properties and different types and grades of the following materials. Give examples of the properties that make each material good or bad for watch-making, from a quality perspective.**

Materials
steel   glass   aluminium   titanium   gold   plastic   copper   rubber

Properties
water-resistant   abrasion-resistant   corrosion-resistant   shock-resistant   tough
brittle   elastic   durable   heavy   lightweight   thermally stable

16 **In small groups, choose a well-known consumer product or appliance and discuss it from a quality perspective. How suitable are the materials used? How good is the product, compared with others sold by competitors?**

UNIT 3

Components and assemblies

- Describing component shapes and features
- Explaining and assessing manufacturing techniques
- Explaining jointing and fixing techniques
- Describing positions of assembled components

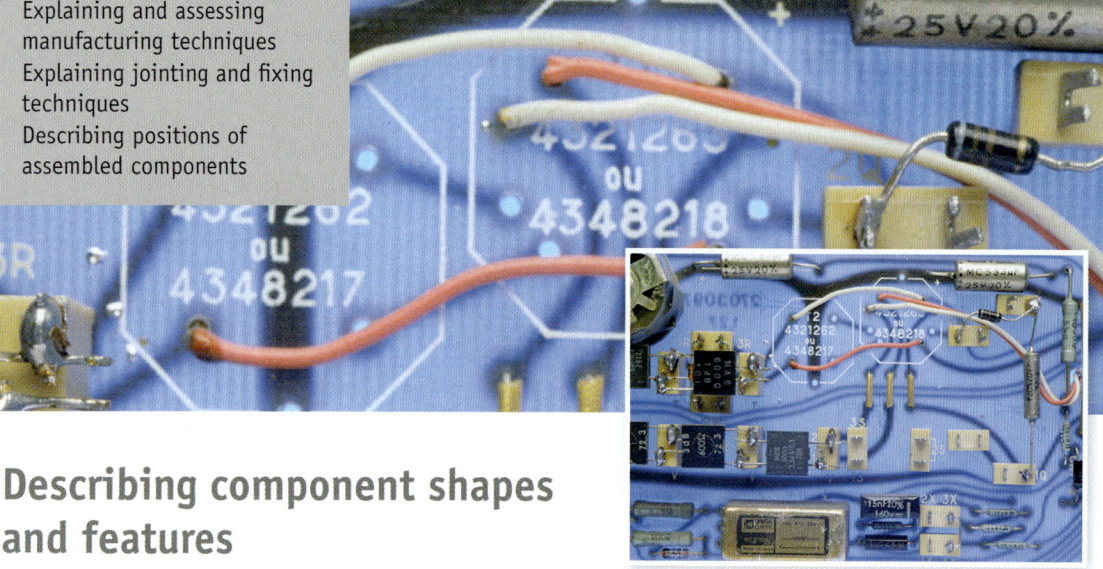

Describing component shapes and features

1   What do you know about the electrical plugs and sockets used in different countries? In pairs, describe some specific designs.

2   a   ▶3.1 Jan, a project manager for a firm that manufactures electrical plugs and sockets, is briefing some of his engineering colleagues. Listen to the briefing and summarise the aim of the project.

   b   In pairs, discuss what is meant by *profile of the pins* and *standard configuration*.

   c   ▶3.2 Erin, an engineer with the same company, is describing different electrical plug and socket formats during the briefing. Listen and match the descriptions (1–6) to the pictures (a–f).

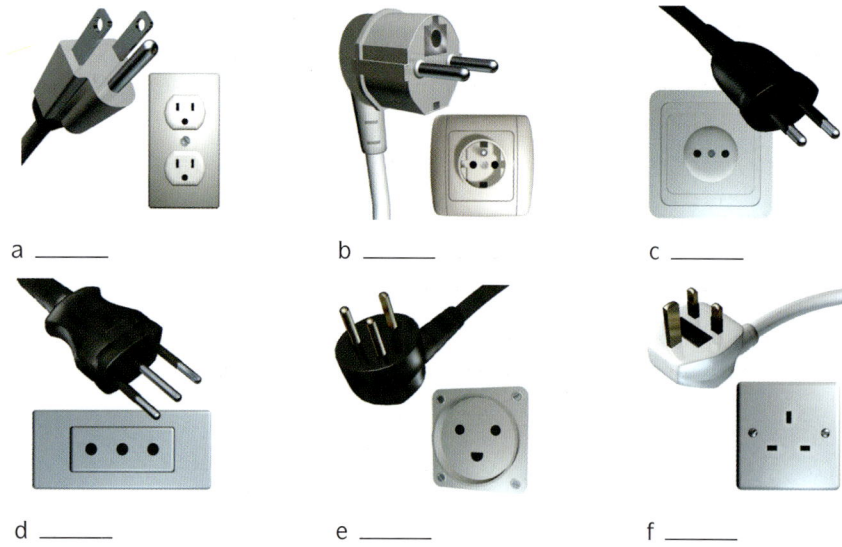

a _____   b _____   c _____

d _____   e _____   f _____

d Complete the following phrases from the descriptions using adjectives based on the words in brackets.

1 ... there are _circular_ pins for live and neutral. (circle)
2 ... the earth slot's got a flat base with one side _____ over to form a semi-circle. (round)
3 This one has _____ blades for live, neutral and earth ... (rectangle)
4 ... it has a _____ slot to receive the earth pin. (cylinder)
5 ... the pins are arranged in _____ configuration. (line)
6 ... they're laid out in _____ configuration. (triangle)

e ▶3.3 Listen and underline the stressed syllable in each of the following words.

rectangle	rectangular	triangle	triangular
cylinder	cylindrical	line	linear

3 a ▶3.4 Listen to a longer description from the meeting. Which picture (a–f) in Exercise 2c does Erin describe?

b Complete the following extracts from the description using the correct form of the words in the box.

flush with   groove   hole   pin   recess   ridge   set back

1 ... there's a circular slot at the top. It's obviously a blind __hole__ , it doesn't go right through.
2 ... there are two plastic _____ , one on either side of the plug casing, and they slot into corresponding _____ at each side of the socket. In addition, the centre of the socket is _____ . So rather than being
_____ the front of the socket, on the same face, the circular area that receives the plug is _____ from the surrounding casing ...
3 These covers only open when pressure is applied to both by the two _____ of the plug simultaneously.

c In pairs, describe the different plug and socket formats in the pictures in Exercise 2c.

4 a ▶3.5 Andy and Karin, two electrical engineers, are evaluating a plug and socket format in Exercise 2c. Listen to the conversation and make notes of the advantages and disadvantages of the following features.

1 Plug slots into a recess in the socket:
Advantages _____
Disadvantages _____
2 Covers protect live and neutral slots:
Advantages _____
Disadvantages _____

b In pairs, discuss the advantages and disadvantages of the plug and socket formats in Exercise 2c. Use the following phrases from the conversation.

an advantage/disadvantage of this format is ...   another advantage/disadvantage is ...
the problem with this system is ...   this (shape/format/feature) stops ... from ... -ing
this (shape/format/feature) allows it to / helps it to / makes it easy to / makes it difficult to ...

Explaining and assessing manufacturing techniques

5 In pairs, think of some examples of machining operations that are often used in manufacturing involving metalworking.

6 a ▶3.6 Evan, a sales engineer with a metal fabrication company, is showing Mr Barrett, a new customer, around their plant. Listen to the conversation and mark the statements True (T) or False (F).

1 The company specialises in sheet metal working.
2 The company does a lot of metal casting.
3 Metal bashing is a precise technical term for hammering.
4 Drills and milling machines are always noisy.
5 Grinding is a process that uses abrasives.
6 The press is used for shearing metal.

b Complete the following training material for graduate engineers using the words in the box.

| Drilling   Flame-cutting   Milling   Sawing   Shearing |

MANUFACTURING TECHNIQUE EVALUATION: CUTTING OPERATIONS

Key factors in determining the most appropriate cutting technique are: material characteristics (notably hardness, and thermal and electrical properties), component thickness, component shape and complexity, required edge quality, and production volume. Select cutting options below for a detailed analysis of techniques.

CUTTING OPTIONS

(1) _____ : abrasive cutting, removing a kerf of material. Includes cutting with toothed blades and abrasive wheels. ◀More ....▶

(2) _____ : use of pressure on smooth-edged blades for guillotining and punching. ◀More ....▶

(3) _____ : removal of material across the full diameter of a hole, or using hole-saws for cutting circumferential kerfs. ◀More ....▶

(4) _____ : removal of surface layers with multiple cutting wheel passes. ◀More ....▶

(5) _____ : using oxy fuel (oxygen + combustible gas, often acetylene). ◀More ....▶

c Complete the following definitions using the words in the box.

| abrasive wheel   guillotine   hole-saw   kerf   punch   toothed blade |

1 A __punch__ makes holes by applying pressure to shear the material.
2 A _____ makes straight cuts by applying pressure to shear the material.
3 A _____ is the width of the saw cut.
4 A _____ has sharp edges for cutting or milling.
5 A _____ has a hard, rough surface for cutting or grinding.
6 A _____ cuts a circular piece to remove an intact core of material.

7 a Read the following extract of promotional literature from a leading producer of ultra-high-pressure (UHP) waterjet cutting machines. In pairs, explain the phrases in bold.

≋ **Flow**

What makes waterjets such a popular cutting option? Water jets require few **secondary operations**, produce **net-shaped parts** with no **heat-affected zone**, heat distortion, or **mechanical stresses** caused by other cutting methods, can cut with a **narrow kerf**, and can provide better usage of raw material since parts can be **tightly nested**. As a result of the FlowMaster™ PC control system and intuitive operation, waterjets are extremely easy to use. Typically, operators can be trained in hours and are producing high-quality parts in hours. Additionally, waterjets can cut virtually any material, leaving a satin-smooth edge.

b ▶3.7 Evan is talking to Mr Barrett about UHP waterjet cutting. Listen to the conversation and match the phrases in the box to the extracts (1–4).

heat-affected zone	mechanical stresses	narrow kerf	net-shaped parts

Extract 1 _____   Extract 3 _____

Extract 2 _____   Extract 4 _____

c Complete the following extracts from the conversation by underlining the correct phrases.
1 *So they are **especially good when** / **not so good when** you have intricate shapes.*
2 *Saw blades are obviously **perfect when** / **useless when** you're cutting curved shapes.*
3 *… sawing is **the ideal solution** / **not the best solution** if you want to avoid altering the material.*
4 *… it's **ideal for** / **totally unsuitable for** metals.*

8 In pairs, assess the different cutting techniques in terms of
● shape/size of cut ● material types/characteristics ● cut width/quality.
Use the phrases in the box.

> ideal/perfect/especially good for + -ing   the ideal/perfect solution for
> not particularly suitable / not so good if you need …
> not the best solution if you don't want …   totally unsuitable / useless

Cutting techniques	Shape/size of cut
drilling with a bit drilling with a hole-saw flame-cutting grinding guillotining milling punching sawing waterjet cutting	angular blind holes curved large small straight thick thin through holes

Material types/characteristics
ceramics   metals   plastics   timber   hard   tough brittle

Cut width/quality
heat-affected zone   narrow kerfs   no kerf   rough edges smooth edges   wide kerfs

Explaining jointing and fixing techniques

9 In pairs, think of some examples of ways of joining materials together.

10 a ▶3.8 Pedro, a purchasing manager with a kitchen appliance manufacturer, is talking to Alicia, a sales manager from one of their main suppliers. Listen to the conversation and answer the following questions.

1 What objective does Pedro describe regarding his company's relationship with suppliers?
2 What is Alicia concerned about?
3 How does he respond to her concerns?

b Complete the following table using the words in the box.

> adhesive ~~bolt~~ clip rivet screw weld

Mechanical fixings	Non-mechanical fixings
_____bolt_____	_____
_____	_____
_____	

c Label the photos (1–6) with the words in Exercise 10b.

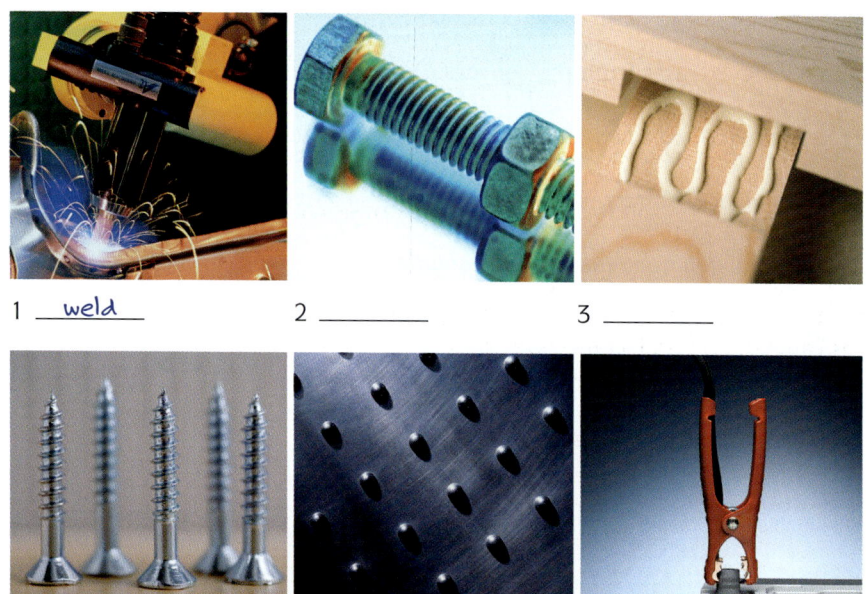

1 ___weld___   2 _____   3 _____

4 _____   5 _____   6 _____

d Match the types of connection in the box to the following groups.

> bolting bonding ~~connecting~~ fixing gluing joining riveting welding

1 _connecting_ _____ _____ = describes any kind of connection.
2 _____ _____ = describes mechanical connections only.
3 _____ _____ _____ = describes non-mechanical connections only.

11 a Complete the following questions using the words in the box.

each other   on   onto   to   together

1 How can we fix these two components _____ ?
2 How can we fix these two components to _____ ?
3 How can we fix this component _____ ?
4 How can we fix this component _____ / _____ this component?

b Complete the following training web page using the words in Exercise 11a.

MANUFACTURING TECHNIQUE EVALUATION: JOINTS AND FIXINGS

The most suitable method of joining components depends on many factors, which extend beyond the obvious issue of required strength.

- Will the joint need to be disconnected in the future? If a part is bolted (1) _____ , it can obviously be removed at a later date. If two components are bonded to (2) _____ with strong adhesive, or welded (3) _____ then subsequent removal will clearly be more difficult. More....

- What external factors might affect the joint? Water or heat can weaken adhesive joints. And no matter how tightly nuts are screwed (4) _____ bolts, vibration can cause them to work loose over time. More....

- How quality-sensitive is the jointing technique? Components are rarely joined (5) _____ each other in ideal conditions. Inadequately tightened fixings, improperly prepared surfaces, or flawed welds are inevitable. How could such imperfections affect the joint negatively? More....

c In pairs, answer the following questions using the information on the web page in Exercise 11b.

1 What are the main advantage and disadvantage of mechanical fixings?
2 What is the main disadvantage of non-mechanical jointing?
3 What issues can negatively affect mechanical fixings and non-mechanical joints?

12 a In pairs, discuss the following jointing techniques used in aircraft and say how the parts are fixed together.

1 Early aircraft: timber frame / adhesive or screws
2 Modern jet aircraft: alloy body panels / rivets
3 Aircraft cabins: seats/floor/bolts
4 Aircraft cockpit: windshield/fuselage/adhesive

b Your company has launched a competition for its engineers to build a homemade model glider that is as cheap as possible to assemble. In pairs, discuss what types of materials and joints you could use.

Describing positions of assembled components

13 **a** In pairs, read the title of the article and suggest ways of making a garden chair fly. Discuss any potential problems.

b Read the article and match the questions (a–d) to the paragraphs (1–4).

a How did the actual flight differ from the one that was planned? _____
b What incidents occurred just before and just after the landing? _____
c What is said about the modern equivalent of this type of activity? _____
d What components were used to assemble the flying machine? _____

CRAZY BUT TRUE: LARRY WALTERS AND THE FLYING GARDEN CHAIR

1 On July 2, 1982, a Californian truck driver named Larry Walters sat outside his house on a garden chair. To say that he was out to get some air is an understatement, for projecting above him a cluster of ropes was tied to 42 helium-filled weather balloons. Anchor ropes, situated underneath the chair, were fastened around the bumper of his car, which was positioned just below the makeshift flying machine.

2 Mr Walters intended to climb gently to an altitude of a few hundred feet, before drifting slowly out of town and across country. He then planned to use an airgun to shoot some balloons and descend gradually to earth. But as the helium gas contained within the balloons warmed up in the summer sun, it progressively generated more lift. When the anchor ropes were released, the self-assembly airship shot up like a rocket. Too shocked to reach for the pistol inserted in his pocket, the first-time pilot held on for life. In just a few minutes, Larry Walters was 16,000 feet above the ground, floating over the city of Long Beach. A short time later, there were further complications; he suddenly found himself inside controlled airspace, adjacent to Long Beach Airport. The occupants of passing Delta Airlines and TWA aircraft looked on at the curious spectacle outside, as wide-eyed as the garden chair pilot hovering beside them.

3 Eventually, after managing to shoot some balloons, Mr Walters descended safely to earth despite an anchor rope, which was still suspended beneath the chair, getting tangled with a power line located alongside the landing site (in someone's garden). He was immediately arrested by waiting police officers, and was later fined for breaking Federal aviation laws.

4 Today, cluster ballooning, while still a fairly marginal sport, is steadily starting to gain in popularity.

c Answer the questions in Exercise 13b.

14 **a** Label the diagrams using the prepositions in the box.

above adjacent to alongside around below beneath beside inside outside over underneath within

a ▢ • _____ _above_ _____

b ▢ • _____ _____ _____

c ▢ • _____ _____ _____

d ▭ _____

e ▱ • _____

f ▱ • _____

b Complete the following sentences about the flying garden chair using the prepositions in the box. Check your answers against the text in Exercise 13b.

in   above   around   beneath   within

1   Projecting _____ the chair was a cluster of ropes, tied to 42 helium-filled weather balloons.
2   Anchor ropes were fastened _____ the bumper of the car.
3   Larry Walters had an airgun inserted _____ his pocket.
4   The helium contained _____ the balloons warmed up in the sun.
5   After takeoff, the anchor ropes remained suspended _____ the chair.

c Complete the following descriptions of how the garden chair airship was assembled by underlining the correct words.

1   A quantity of helium gas was <u>contained</u>/suspended inside each balloon.
2   A tube was **inserted/projected** inside the openings of the balloons, to inflate them.
3   The balloons were **situated/suspended** over the chair, in a large cluster.
4   The chair was **contained/suspended** under the balloons by ropes.
5   Arm rests, **contained/located** beside the pilot, at each side, helped to hold him in place.
6   The landing gear, **inserting/projecting** below the seat, consisted, simply, of the chair legs.
7   The pilot was **positioned/projected** underneath the balloons, so his weight was low down.

d Which two other words have the same meaning as *positioned*?

contained   fastened   inserted   located   projected   situated   suspended

15   **a** In pairs, look at the photo and describe how you think the cluster balloon is assembled from the following components.

bags   balloons   helium   nylon ropes   nylon straps   paragliding harness
plastic cable   sand/water ballast   ties   tape

b ▶3.9 Eva and Lenny, two engineers working for an extreme sports equipment manufacturer, are discussing cluster ballooning. Listen to the conversation and summarise what they say about the following issues.

1   assembly time
2   how plastic cable ties are used
3   a tree structure
4   how water bags are used

5   the advantage of tying each individual balloon
6   the problem of using a net to contain the balloons

c In pairs, discuss ways of overcoming the problems mentioned in the conversation. How could cluster ballooning be made more accessible to a mass market? What other equipment/assemblies could be used?

UNIT 4 Engineering design

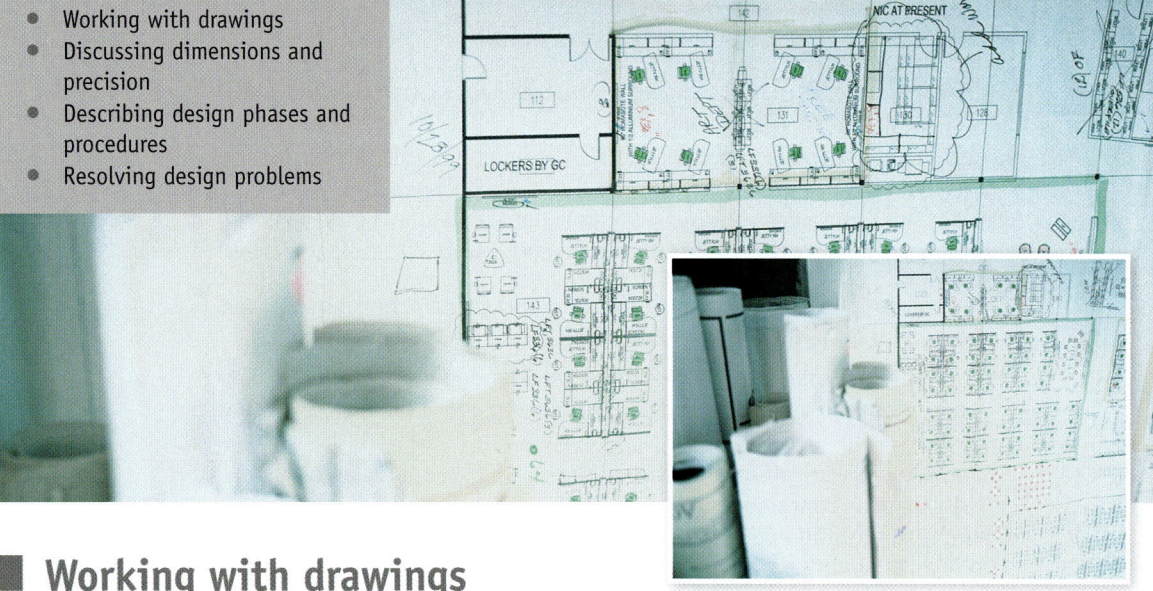

- Working with drawings
- Discussing dimensions and precision
- Describing design phases and procedures
- Resolving design problems

Working with drawings

1 In pairs, discuss the different types of design information needed on a complex engineering project, such as the construction of a large cruise ship. How many different drawings do you think might be produced for such a project? How would they be organised and categorised?

2 **a** ▶ 4.1 Joe, a technician at a shipyard, is talking to Linda, one of his engineering colleagues in the design office. He is asking about some information which he can't find on any of the drawings. Listen to the conversation and answer the following questions.

1 What area of the ship are they discussing?
2 What does the technician need to know?

b Complete the following definitions using the types of drawing in the box.

> cross-section   elevation   exploded view   note   ~~plan~~   schematic
> specification

1 A ___plan___ gives a view of the whole deck, from above.
2 An _____ gives a view of all the panels, from the front.
3 An _____ gives a deconstructed view of how the panels are fixed together.
4 A _____ gives a cutaway view of the joint between two panels.
5 A _____ gives a simplified representation of a network of air ducts.
6 A _____ gives a brief description or a reference to another related drawing.
7 A _____ gives detailed written technical descriptions of the panels.

c Which two types of drawing in Exercise 2b are examples of general arrangement drawings, and which two are examples of detail drawings?

d Read the following technical questions that came up during the shipbuilding project and decide which type of drawing is required to answer each question.

1 How many panels are there altogether on this wall? _____
2 What profile are these hollow beams: rectangular or circular? _____
3 What are the positions of all the floodlights around the deck perimeter? _____
4 How many branches come off the main sprinkler supply pipe? _____
5 How do all the internal components of the fan unit fit together? _____

3 a What is meant by *scale* on a drawing? In pairs, explain how a scale rule, like the one shown in the picture, is used.

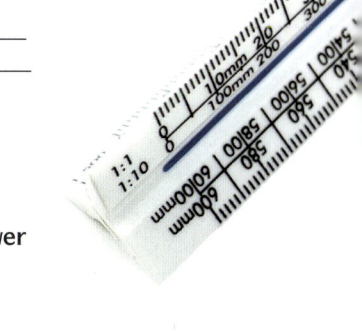

b ▶4.2 After receiving the drawings for the panels, Joe is now discussing some details with Pavel, a colleague. Listen to the conversation and answer the following questions.

1 What piece of information is not shown on the drawing?
2 What *golden rule* is mentioned?

c Complete the following extracts from the conversation and explain what is meant by each one.

1 *Is this drawing _____ scale?*
2 *It's one _____ five.*
3 *… you shouldn't scale _____ drawings …*
4 *… it's actual size, on a _____-scale drawing …*

4 You are engineers on a project to design the metal handrail that will run around the perimeter of the top, outdoor deck of a large cruise ship. In pairs, discuss what drawings you will need to produce for manufacturing and installation with regard to the following issues:

- the types of view that will be required and what each one will show
- the approximate scale of different drawings and views
- what written information you will need to provide in the specification.

5 You are going to provide design information to enable a production team to manufacture a product or appliance you know well. Make a list of some of the drawings that will be needed, noting what each one will show.

Discussing dimensions and precision

6 a In pairs, discuss what is meant by *precision* and *accuracy*.

b Read the technical advice web page and answer the following questions.

1 How is a superflat floor different from an ordinary concrete floor?
2 What accuracy can be achieved with ordinary slabs, and with superflat slabs?
3 What problem is described in high bay warehouses?

Superflat Floors: FAQ

What is a superflat floor?

Compacting and finishing the surface of wet concrete is an inherently imprecise process. For an ordinary concrete slab to be laid within tolerance, engineers can only realistically expect the surface to be finished to plus or minus 5mm. By contrast, superflat concrete floors are finished to meet extremely close tolerances, being accurate to within 1mm across their upper surface.

Where are superflat floors used?

Floor surfaces with extremely tight tolerances are frequently specified in warehouses where Automated Guided Vehicles operate. Uneven floors are especially problematic in high bay warehouses, which use automated forklifts with a vertical reach of 30 metres or more. At such a height, slight variations in floor level are amplified in the form of vertical tilt, causing inaccurate manoeuvring at high level. If these variations are outside tolerance they can lead to collisions with racking elements, or cause items to be dropped from pallets.

---

c In pairs, discuss what is meant by *tolerance* in the context of dimensions and precision.

d Complete the following expressions from the web page which are used to describe tolerances.

1 _____ tolerance (inside the limits of a given tolerance)
2 _____ or _____ 5mm (+ / − 5mm)
3 _____ tolerance (close tolerance)
4 _____ tolerance (not inside the limits of tolerance)

e Complete the following sentences using the expressions in Exercise 6d.

1 The frame's too big for the opening. The opening's the right size, so the frame must be _____ .
2 The total tolerance is 1mm. The permissible variation either side of the ideal is _____ .
3 The engineer specified + / − 5mm for the slab finish, and we got it to + / − 2mm. So it's well _____ .
4 You can't finish concrete to + / − 0.1mm. There's no way you can work to such a _____ .

f In some situations, engineers describe tolerances using *plus or minus*, for example + / − 1mm, and in other situations as *within*, for example *within 1mm*. In pairs, discuss the difference in meaning between these two descriptions, giving examples of situations where each description might be used.

7 a ▶4.3 **Mei, a structural engineer, is talking to Lewis, a project manager, about the floor specification for a manufacturing plant that is currently at design stage. Listen to the conversation and answer the following questions.**

1 What has the client requested with regard to the floor slab?
2 What are free movement floors and defined movement floors?
3 What issue does the engineer discuss regarding quality?
4 What option is discussed involving grinding?
5 What can be done to the reinforcement to permit grinding?

b Complete the following table using the words in the text in Exercise 6b and audioscript 4.3 on page 89.

	Name of dimension	Large dimension	Small dimension
1	What's the _____?	Is it _____?	Is it short?
2	What's the width ?	Is it _____?	Is it narrow?
3	What's the _____?	Is it high ?	Is it low?
4	What's the thickness?	Is it _____?	Is it thin?
5	What's the _____?	Is it deep ?	Is it shallow?

c Mei has done a revised drawing for the floor slab. Read the extract from her email about the new design and complete the message using the correct form of the words in Exercise 7b.

To: Lewis Rosas
Subject: Revised floor slab drawing

Please find attached a revised drawing for the floor slab, now reconfigured for defined movement. In order to accommodate guided vehicles 1 080mm (1) ___wide___ (as specified by the client) we propose a standard (2) _____ of 1 280mm for each superflat lane. At 14.5m, the (3) _____ of the longest lane on the network is within the maximum slab run that can be cast in a single concrete pour, thus avoiding construction joints on straight runs. On curved sections, a standard 8.5m turning radius is used, as per the guided vehicle manufacturer's recommendations.

In order to allow for the eventuality of future grinding, we have located the top layer of reinforcement 10mm deeper below the slab surface. This additional (4) _____ has not, however, been added to the overall slab (5) _____ , which remains 275mm. The reinforcing bars also remain in 12mm diameter. As a result, the levels of wall-mounted process installations – many of which need to be fixed at a precise (6) _____ above finished floor level – are unaffected.

d Which two words in the email relate to circles? What aspects of a circle do they describe?

8 The manufacturing plant in Exercise 7 will be built from a steel frame. The vertical elements of the frame will be Universal Columns (UCs). Look at the section of a UC. In pairs, describe the different dimensions that define a UC profile by explaining what the letters on the section refer to.

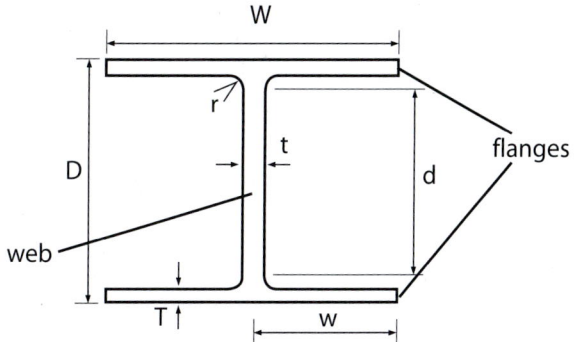

Describing design phases and procedures

9   In pairs, discuss what is meant by a *design process*. In engineering, what are the stages in the development of designs?

10 **a** The following extracts from emails relate to a project to build an indoor ski complex in Australia, using artificial snow. The messages were circulated by an engineer to members of the design team, and to a specialist contractor. Read the emails and, in pairs, answer the following questions. Note that the emails are not in the correct order.

1   What are all the emails about?
2   What different types of documents are mentioned?

a

We now have a full set of working drawings for the main ski lift (attached). These incorporate some amendments requested by the client, which have now been approved. Hard copies have been forwarded to the relevant contractors' premises, for fabrication.

b

I attach a summary of our meeting with the client last Tuesday. It outlines ideas expressed by the client's marketing team, and describes what an experience at the ski complex should be like, from a visitor's point of view. We'll be going through these notes at the project kick-off meeting next Thursday, to clarify the design brief, so please formulate any queries before then.

c

Please find attached a full set of preliminary drawings, as submitted to the client for approval / comments. These are for information only at this stage.

d

Attached are a few rough sketches setting out the overall layout of the ski complex. At this point, these are initial ideas based on the client's suggestions and the approximate dimensions specified in the design brief. I look forward to any feedback by the end of this week.

e

Please note that dwg 18A is currently being revised, to resolve problems encountered during assembly of the ski lift. Revision B will be circulated next week. Until the amended drawing is issued, please treat dwg 18A as superseded. If you require specific details urgently, please contact me, and I will arrange for a suitable sketch to be issued.

b Put the emails in the correct sequence.

1 _____   2 _____   3 _____   4 _____   5 _____

c Complete the following definitions using the types of drawing in the box.

design brief   preliminary drawing   sketch   working drawing

1   A _____ is a rough drawing of initial ideas, also used when production problems require engineers to amend design details and issue them to the workforce immediately.
2   A _____ is a written summary intended to specify design objectives.
3   A _____ is an approved drawing used for manufacturing or installation. There is often a need to revise these drawings to resolve production problems. In this case, amended versions are issued to supercede the previous ones.
4   A _____ is a detailed drawing that colleagues and consultants are invited to approve if they accept them, or comment on if they wish to request any changes.

d Find synonyms for the following words in the definitions in Exercise 10c.

1 accept / _approve_
2 amend / _____
3 approximate / _____
4 circulate / _____
5 give feedback / _____
6 replace / update / _____
7 state / _____
8 solve / _____

e In pairs, suggest what needs to be done next in each of the following situations.

1 They've found a problem with drawing 63 on site. The detail we've specified doesn't work.
2 I've done a preliminary design for the duct layout, but the client hasn't seen it yet.
3 I've got a feeling the drawing they have on site isn't the latest one.
4 We've just revised drawing 14. The changes are going to affect three different contractors.
5 This is the client's written design brief. How shall we kick off the design work?

11 a Leo is the ski complex project manager. With design work about to begin, he is meeting senior engineers from the design teams to discuss design coordination. In pairs, explain the items on the meeting agenda and suggest what kinds of issue might be discussed.

b ▶ 4.4 Listen to three extracts from the meeting and match each extract (1–3) to an agenda item (a–c).

1 _____ 2 _____ 3 _____

c ▶ 4.4 Listen again and make notes about the problems discussed in the meeting. In pairs, discuss some possible solutions to the problems.

d ▶ 4.5 Listen to Leo summarising the solutions that have been agreed in the meeting. What has been decided regarding the following points?

1 The decision that the senior engineer in each team must make, regarding drawings
2 The circulation procedure that will be used for each drawing
3 The role of the M&E coordinator in relation to the senior engineers and the project manager
4 The arrangement that will make informal communication easier

e In pairs, discuss how the design procedures discussed in the meeting will work in the following situations.

1 Issuing the first draft of a specialised hydraulic hose drawing for the ski lift
2 Designing an electrical supply system for some water-cooling equipment
3 Revising the connection details between some ski-lift machinery and its concrete foundation

> **Australian Ski complex – Design Coordination Meeting Agenda**
> Tuesday 8th May
> Conference room 9.30am – 11.00am
> To: RN, LG, SB, CW, SH
>
> **Item**
>
> a Design interface (mechanical, electrical)
>
> b Design and information flow procedure (structural, mechanical, electrical)
>
> c Inter-team communication – formal and informal

Resolving design problems

12   In pairs, discuss problems that can arise when different drawings that make up a design are not properly coordinated.

13   **a**   The following records are from the indoor ski complex project. They show correspondence between the design team and construction team. Read through the texts quickly and answer the following questions.

1   What is the general subject of the correspondence?
2   What is meant by *query* and *instruction*?
3   Some queries refer to earlier conversations. Suggest why these have been followed up in writing.
4   What is meant by *dwg* and *dims*?

CONTRACTOR'S QUERY No. 867	ENGINEER'S INSTRUCTION
Following our telephone conversation today, we note that there is a discrepancy between dwgs 76E and 78E, which indicate conflicting dimensions for the width of the roof opening. Please clarify which dimension is correct.	We confirm the correct dimension is on dwg 76E. Please disregard the dims on dwg 78E.
CONTRACTOR'S QUERY No. 868	ENGINEER'S INSTRUCTION
As discussed this morning on site, we confirm there is a clash between the proposed cable tray (dwg E56) and air-conditioning ductwork (now installed as per dwg M118) in the ceiling void at Grid D14. Please advise on an alternative cable route.	Please work to attached sketch S33. Revision of dwg E56 to follow.
CONTRACTOR'S QUERY No. 869	ENGINEER'S INSTRUCTION
A note on dwg 11A specifies black bolts at the base of the ski lift cable support. This contradicts the specification, which states that all joints to comprise High Strength Friction Grip bolts. We propose using HSFG fixings at this location.	Please provide further details of the HSFG bolts you are proposing.
CONTRACTOR'S QUERY No. 870	ENGINEER'S INSTRUCTION
Further to Query 869, the proposed HSFG bolts are as per those specified for all other bolted joints on the ski lift supports. Our intention is to use a single bolt spec to facilitate assembly.	Approved.

b   Read the correspondence in detail. Write the query numbers in Exercise 13a next to the descriptions (1–5). You will need to refer to some queries more than once.

1   An installation that won't fit, as components are in each other's way   _868_
2   A response from the engineer asking for more information   _____
3   Queries that suggest a solution, which will require the engineer's approval

   _____   _____
4   Requests to the engineer to instruct the contractor or make something clear.

   _____   _____
5   Separate documents referring to details that don't correspond with each other   _____   _____   _____

c Complete the following pairs of sentences using the verbs in the box.

advise   clarify   clash   propose   request

1 The components are in each other's way. = The components _____ .
2 Please ask for more information. = Please _____ more information.
3 Can I suggest a solution to the problem? = Can I _____ a solution?
4 Please instruct the supplier to send the parts to this address. = Please _____ the supplier.
5 Any conflicting details must be queried. = You must _____ any conflicting details.

14 a In pairs, look at the following plan and sections from a drawing on the ski complex project, showing steelwork details on part of a ski lift. Examine how the rectangular plate is bolted to the T profile below it. Can you find the discrepancy between the details, and the clash preventing the connection from being assembled?

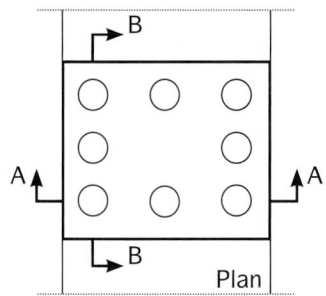

Plan

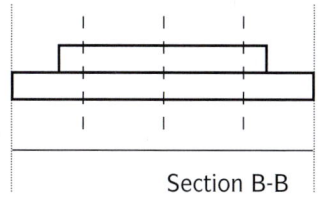

Section B-B

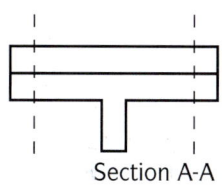

Section A-A

b Chen, a technician, is explaining the problem in Exercise 14a to Ron, an engineer. Complete the conversation using the words in the box.

alternative   as per   clarify   clash   confirm   contradicts   discrepancy   propose

Chen: *There's a (1) discrepancy between these details that you might be able to (2) _____ straight away. On the plan of this plate, it shows eight bolts. But on section A, here, there are no bolts shown in the middle. So there would only be six, which obviously (3) _____ the plan. But as you can see, this plate's going to be bolted to a T profile. So we couldn't put a row of bolts down the middle, because they'd (4) _____ with the flange running along the middle of the T. So I'd (5) _____ just going for two rows of bolts. The (6) _____ would be to redesign the T section, which would obviously be a bigger job.*

Ron: *Yes. Let's go for two rows of bolts, (7) _____ the sections.*

Chen: *OK, fine. Will you send an email to (8) _____ that?*

c ▶4.6 Listen to the conversation and check your answers to Exercise 14b. How does the explanation compare with your description of the problem?

d Write an email from Ron to Chen, confirming the revision agreed in the discussion above.

UNIT 5 Breaking point

- Describing types of technical problem
- Assessing and interpreting faults
- Describing the causes of faults
- Discussing repairs and maintenance

Describing types of technical problem

1 In pairs, discuss the technical challenges of endurance car races like the Le Mans 24 Hours sports car race.

2 a ▶5.1 Sabino, an engineer with a sports car racing team, is giving a talk to some of his team's sponsors at a test session. Listen to the talk and answer the following questions.

1 What saying emphasises the importance of reliability?
2 What expression refers to things that can cause failures?
3 What expression describes damage caused by normal use?

b ▶5.1 In the talk, Sabino names five engineering enemies. Complete the following list. Listen again and check your answers.

1 h_____ = high temperatures
2 p_____ = loads from expanding gases or liquids
3 v_____ = continuous high-frequency movement or shaking
4 s_____ = sudden impacts
5 a_____ = damage to surfaces caused by friction

c In pairs, suggest which engineering enemies in Exercise 2b can be the most problematic for each of the following car parts.

1 chassis	4 suspension	7 wings
2 engine	5 brakes	8 cooling system
3 gearbox and clutch	6 tyres	9 nuts and bolts

3 a ▶5.2 Listen to Sabino talking about some technical problems the team have had at the test and mark the following statements True (T) or False (F).

1 Some liquid was lost from a pipe.
2 A car lost all its coolant with the engine still running.
3 A car's engine stopped on the circuit.
4 Some tyres were damaged.
5 A wheel nut fell off a car on the circuit.
6 A car's suspension was broken.

b Complete the following extracts from the talk using the words in the box.

> bend   blocking   crack   jam   snap

1 … you don't want anything _____ the airflow to the radiators.
2 … they had a wheel nut _____ , it wouldn't turn.
3 … he didn't hit the barriers and _____ the suspension or _____ it completely.
4 … it didn't _____ the tub – the chassis.

c Complete more extracts from the talk using the correct form of a verb in box 1 and a word in box 2.

> **1**
> blow   clog   cut   leak   run   wear   ~~work~~

> **2**
> ~~loose~~   up   out

1 … a nut _underline{worked}_ _underline{loose}_ on a radiator pipe, which resulted in coolant liquid _____ _____ .
2 … he switched off before the system had _____ _____ of coolant.
3 … the engine _____ _____ on one of the corners.
4 … the openings in the side pods always _____ _____ with dirt.
5 The tyres weren't close to _____ _____ …
6 … the radiator problem didn't cause the engine to _____ _____ .

d ▶5.2 Listen again and check your answers to Exercises 3b and 3c.

e Read the following comments made by race team technicians. Complete the following sentences using the correct form of words in Exercises 3b and 3c.

1 There's smoke and flames pouring out of the engine. It's _underline{blown up}_ .
2 There's a pool of oil under the car. Something's _____ .
3 This cylinder head bolt won't loosen. It's _____ .
4 The air filter's full of dirt. It's completely _____ .
5 This wing support's been moving about. The bolts have _____ .
6 Something's stopping the oil flow. The pipe might be _____ .
7 Are you sure that pushrod's straight? It looks as if it's _____ .
8 We'll need to change these brake pads. They're nearly _____ .
9 There's hardly any fuel left in the car. In another lap, we'll _____ .

4 Read the technical facts about the Italian motor racing circuit, Monza, and summarise how the track is different from most others.
In pairs, discuss the technical problems that racing cars could have at Monza as a result of the factors described in the text.

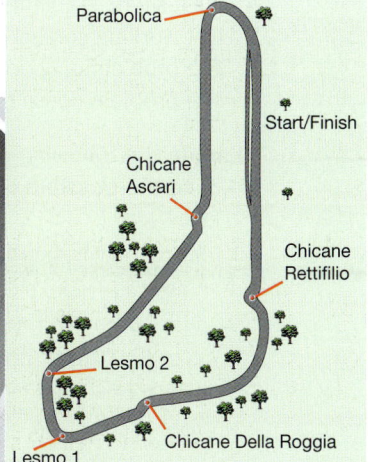

The circuit is characterised by long straights and chicanes. This means the cars' engines are at full throttle for over 75% of the lap, a higher percentage than most other circuits.
The track requires heavier-than-average braking over a given lap, as the cars repeatedly decelerate at the end of some of the world's fastest straights for the slow chicanes.
The chicanes are lined by rugged kerbs. Riding over these hard is crucial for fast laps.
The long straights require small wings for minimum drag. This means lower downforce, resulting in lower grip on corners and under braking, and less stability over bumps.
The main high-speed corners Lesmo 1, Lesmo 2 and Parabolica are all right turns.
Parts of the circuit are surrounded by trees, which means leaves can be blown onto the track.

Assessing and interpreting faults

5 a In pairs, discuss a technical problem you've experienced with a device, equipment or vehicle. Describe the fault, and how you tried to solve the problem.

b Read the training notes for telephone helpline staff working for a manufacturer of mining plant. In pairs, discuss what each point means.

> *Problem-solving checklist*
> 1 *User's observations:*
>   *- nature of fault*
>   *- circumstances of fault*
>   *- external factors*
> 2 *Process of elimination*
> 3 *Identify the failure*
> 4 *Determine action and urgency*

6 a ▶5.3 **Mr Rooney, an engineer at a quarry firm, is talking to Al, a helpline consultant, about a technical problem with a diesel engine. Listen to the conversation and answer the following questions.**

1 What does the warning message say?
2 What external factor is discussed as a possible cause?
3 Why is this possible cause eliminated?
4 In what circumstances does the fault occur?
5 What does the consultant identify as the most likely cause?
6 What action is required, and how urgent is it?

b Match the words in the box to their synonyms in the sentences (1–7).

> defect   defective   ~~fault~~   faulty   intermittently   major   minor   properly   systematically

1 There's a **problem**. __fault__ / _____
2 Perhaps something in the fuel injection system is **wrong**. _____ / _____
3 It's a **serious** problem. _____
4 It's a **slight** problem. _____
5 Is it working **correctly**? _____
6 The problem only occurs **from time to time**. _____
7 The problem doesn't occur **every time**. _____

c Al made the following notes about three engine problems. Match the faults (1–3) to the possible causes (a–c).

> 1 Starter motor sometimes works, sometimes doesn't. Engine is 9 years old.
> 2 Distribution belt failed. Engine blew. Belt replaced recently – almost new
> 3 New engine. Runs for 20 mins, then temp. gauge always goes into red, and engine cuts out (safety override)

> a Cooling system problem. Fan? Water pump?
> b Electrical contact problem. Loose connection?
> c Manufacturing defect? Incorrect fitting? Not wear

d In pairs, describe the problems in Exercise 6c using the following phrases.

> a faulty part   a sudden problem   a systematic problem   an installation problem
> an intermittent problem   caused by wear and tear   It's / It was …   It's / It was probably …
> Perhaps it's / it was …   This is / was a …

e Complete the following table using the phrases in the box from the conversation.

> I doubt it's   it can't be   it could be   it might be   ~~it must be~~   it sounds like it's

1 It's certainly / _it must be_	
2 It's probably / _____	
3 It's possibly / _____ / _____	a problem with …
4 It's probably not / _____	
5 It's certainly not / _____	

f ▶5.3 Complete the following extracts from the conversation using phrases in Exercise 2e. Listen again and check your answers.

1 *Obviously,* _it must be_ *some sort of defect in the fuel injection system.*
2 *So _____ a software problem.*
3 *… maybe _____ a defective sensor.*
4 *Presumably, _____ anything too serious.*
5 *_____ water, then, if the fuel went in directly from a delivery.*
6 *_____ a faulty fuel pre-heater.*

7 a In pairs, analyse the problem described below. Underline the words in the box that describe it.

> major   minor   sudden   systematic   intermittent

> **The problem**
> The driver of a dump truck, which operates in a quarry, has noticed that the truck's diesel engine is slightly down on power. The problem has become progressively worse over several weeks. Apart from the power loss, the engine is performing consistently, with no misfiring and no overheating. The degree of power loss remains constant throughout a given period of use, from starting the engine to turning it off. No increase in fuel consumption has been noted.

b Read the notes and assess the possible causes of the problem in Exercise 7a using the words in Exercises 6d and 6e.

> *Possible causes of the engine problem*
> * *water in the fuel supply*
> * *a lubrication problem*
> * *a clogged fuel filter*
> * *a blockage in the exhaust system*
> * *a compression leak from the piston cylinders*

Describing the causes of faults

8 Look at the following strategies for preventing and dealing with technical problems in aviation. In pairs, discuss what is meant by the following terms and how they are used by engineers and pilots.

1 checklists
2 standard procedures
3 back-up installations
4 planned maintenance

9 a Read the article on the right and answer the following questions.

1 How did the problem start?
2 What were the initial, unseen consequences?
3 What were the subsequent consequences?

b Complete the sequence of events that followed the fuel leak on the Airbus A330 using the extracts (a–d).

"We have a problem"
The true story of Air Transat Flight 236.

The chain of events began during routine maintenance work on an Air Transat Airbus A330. An incorrect hydraulic pipe was fitted to the right-hand engine. The component was oversized, leaving inadequate clearance with an adjacent fuel line. Subsequently, the two pipes rubbed together, causing the fuel line to wear progressively. The problem went undetected, until the night of August 24, 2001, at 35,000 feet above the Atlantic. With Flight 236 en route from Toronto to Lisbon, carrying 306 people, the fuel line ruptured, resulting in a major leak. Less than two hours later, the aircraft was completely out of fuel, gliding silently through the night sky …

04:38 The flight data recorder registered an abnormal increase in fuel consumption. At this stage, however, this slight anomaly was insufficient to cause warning lights to come on to alert the crew to any imminent danger.

04:58 _____

05:33 A warning message came up, alerting the crew to an imbalance between the amount of fuel in each wing tank. Initially, the problem was thought to be an instrument malfunction. But further analysis by the crew revealed that the amount of fuel remaining in the right tank was significantly below the planned quantity.

05:36 _____

05:45 As a precaution, the crew decided to divert to the nearest airport - the Lajes military airbase in the Azores.

06:13 _____

06:26 ENG 2 FAIL appeared, and the left engine cut out. Having completely run out of fuel, and with both engines now down, the Airbus A330 was gliding, descending at 2,000 feet per minute.

06:27 _____

06:46 With the airport in sight, the landing gear was lowered manually. The pilot then performed a series of spectacular zigzag manoeuvres to slow the plane down as much as possible. The aircraft touched down on the runway at 370 km/h – exceeding the standard approach speed by over 100 km/h. The pilot applied emergency braking, causing several tyres to blow out and catch fire. But the plane stopped safely, well before the end of the runway.

---

a An alarm sounded, a red master warning lit up and the message ENG 1 FAIL came up on the screen. Seconds later, the right engine flamed out, due to insufficient fuel.

b During a routine instrument check, the crew noticed a disproportionate amount of oil had been used by each engine. Oil pressure and temperature readings for each engine were also irregular, but the levels were found to be within acceptable parameters.

c As the aircraft was now powerless and potentially uncontrollable, an emergency ram air turbine was deployed automatically to generate back-up electrical power for the fly-by-wire controls and instruments. However, with the main hydraulics shut down, the flaps and spoilers used to slow the plane before and after landing were inoperable. The co-pilot calculated the plane could remain airborne for 15–20 minutes, and that Lajes airbase was an estimated 20 minutes away.

d The crew decided to take action to correct the anomaly, opening a cross-feed valve to transfer fuel from the left tank to the right tank.

c Make opposites of the following words using the prefixes in the box.

ab-　dis-　im-　in- (x4)　ir-　mal-　over-　un-

1　correct　_incorrect_
2　undersized　_____
3　adequate　_____
4　detected　_____
5　normal　_____
6　sufficient　_____

7　proportionate　_____
8　regular　_____
9　balance　_____
10　function　_____
11　operable　_____

d Complete the following sentences using the words in Exercise 9c. Sometimes more than one word is possible.

1　The temperature gauge was faulty. That's why it was giving _____ readings.
2　The shaft was thinner than it should have been, so its strength was _____ .
3　The power output from the motor varies. We don't understand why it's _____ .
4　The bolt's _____ . It's too big to fit into the hole.
5　The machine's not working as it should. There's some kind of _____ .
6　The braking force on both front wheels should be the same. There shouldn't be an _____ .
7　The fault was _____ . None of the maintenance technicians had noticed it.
8　The control panel isn't working, so you can't control the machine. It's totally _____ .

10 a ▶5.4 Julia, an aircraft service technician, is phoning Alan, a colleague, about a problem with the tyres on a plane. Listen to the conversation and mark the statements True (T) or False (F).

1　The tyre pressures on the block being discussed are OK.
2　There is too little air inside some of the tyres.
3　The tyre pressures are the same across the aircraft.
4　The degree of wear across all the tyres is the same.

b Complete the following sentences using words in Exercise 9c to make true sentences about the conversation.

1　The tyre pressures on the block being discussed are _____ .
2　There is _____ air pressure inside some of the tyres.
3　The tyre pressures on that block are _____ to the rest of the aircraft.
4　The wear rate is _____ across all the tyres.

c In pairs, discuss the possible causes of insufficient tyre pressure in general, and the specific problem Julia describes in Exercise 10a, and say why each general cause you discussed is likely or unlikely in this case.

Discussing repairs and maintenance

11 a In pairs, discuss the difference between repairs and maintenance and decide whether the following words relate to repairs, maintenance or both.

> broken   clogged   defective   faulty   worn

b In pairs, compare car maintenance with aircraft maintenance. Which aspects are quite similar and which are very different?

12 a Match the content sections (1–10) of an aircraft service manual to the descriptions (a–j).

Contents

1	Opening and dismantling access panels	[f]
2	Topping up, draining and replacing coolants and lubricants	☐
3	Replacing filters	☐
4	Safely isolating electrical components	☐
5	Safely disconnecting and reconnecting electrical components	☐
6	Mechanical connections to be checked/tightened at each service	☐
7	Parts susceptible to wear/damage, to be examined at each service	☐
8	Sensitive devices to be adjusted at each service	☐
9	Information on non-serviceable parts / sealed units	☐
10	Table of component life spans	☐

a Switching off the power supply
b Making sure certain parts haven't worked loose
c Changing parts that can become clogged
d Adding and changing fluids
e Equipment that needs to be set up precisely
f ~~Taking something to pieces to allow maintenance~~
g Taking parts off and refitting them without danger
h Components that can't be repaired on site
i Details of how long parts are designed to last
j Making sure parts are still in good condition

b Match the verbs (1–10) from Exercise 12a to the definitions (a–j).

1	adjust	a	carry out planned maintenance
2	drain	b	change an old or damaged part
3	disconnect	c	check carefully
4	dismantle	d	empty a liquid
5	examine	e	add more fluid to fill a tank to the recommended level
6	replace	f	set up carefully by making small changes
7	reconnect	g	take apart assembled components
8	service	h	apply the correct torque, for example to loose bolts
9	tighten	i	establish a connection again
10	top up	j	remove or isolate from a circuit or network

13 **a** ▶5.5 A service technician is examining some machinery and talking to a colleague. What does he say about each point on the maintenance checklist?

> *Maintenance Checklist*
> 1   *Coolant level* _____
> 2   *Coolant condition* _____
> 3   *Coolant filter condition* _____
> 4   *Blade wear/damage* _____
> 5   *Blade alignment* _____

b ▶5.5 Listen again. Do you think the technicians are working on an aircraft or on an industrial machine?

c In pairs, discuss what maintenance needs to be carried out on the machinery in Exercise 13a, describing the operations step by step.

14 **a** You work for IPS, a producer of industrial packaging machinery. As a member of the global service team your role is to travel abroad dealing with serious technical problems at your clients' plants. Read the following email from a plant in Helsinki and summarise the problem.

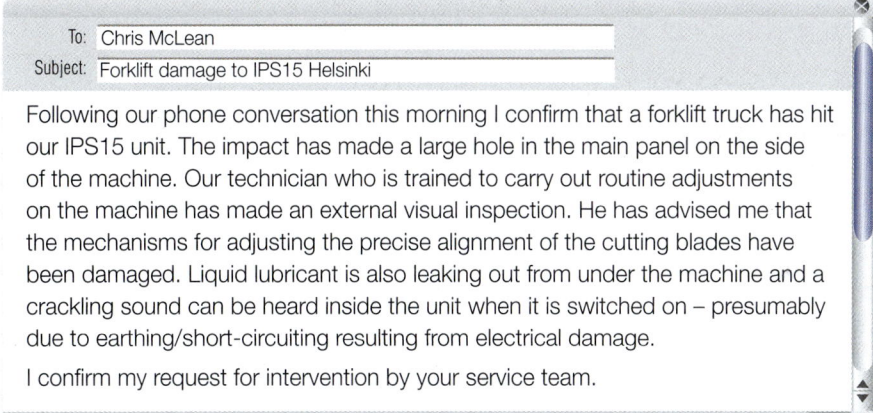

To: Chris McLean
Subject: Forklift damage to IPS15 Helsinki

Following our phone conversation this morning I confirm that a forklift truck has hit our IPS15 unit. The impact has made a large hole in the main panel on the side of the machine. Our technician who is trained to carry out routine adjustments on the machine has made an external visual inspection. He has advised me that the mechanisms for adjusting the precise alignment of the cutting blades have been damaged. Liquid lubricant is also leaking out from under the machine and a crackling sound can be heard inside the unit when it is switched on – presumably due to earthing/short-circuiting resulting from electrical damage.

I confirm my request for intervention by your service team.

b In pairs, describe the sequence of steps you'll need to take to carry out repairs when you arrive in Finland, using the notes to help you.

15 Think back to some repairs or maintenance you did, or had done for you, in the past, for example on a car, bike or domestic appliance. In pairs, explain what servicing or repairs were required, and the main steps involved in carrying them out.

> *IPS15 Helsinki*
> • *internal damage*
> • *old parts*
> • *electrical supply: on / off*
> • *lubricant: in / out*
> • *external panels*
> • *alignment of cutting blades*
> • *test*
> • *new parts*

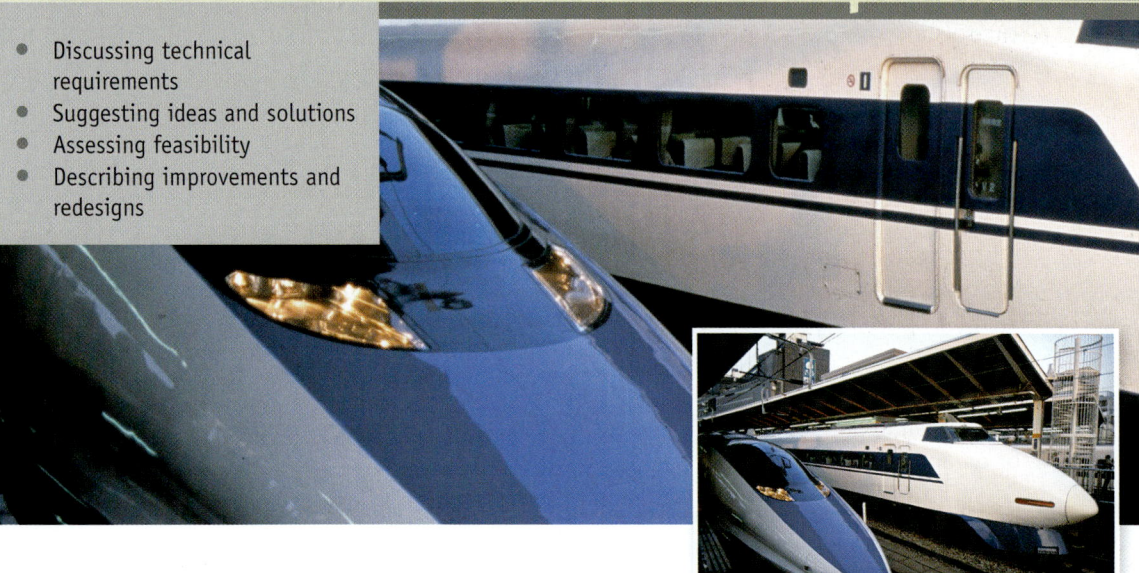

UNIT 6 Technical development

- Discussing technical requirements
- Suggesting ideas and solutions
- Assessing feasibility
- Describing improvements and redesigns

Discussing technical requirements

1 What is *needs analysis*? In pairs, discuss why the following factors are important in needs analysis, giving examples of products and installations.

> budget   capacity   dimensions   layout   looks   performance
> regulations   timescale

2 a ▶6.1 Claudia, an engineer, is asking Kevin and Dave, the managers of a fun park, about their requirements for a proposed space module simulator called *Mars Lander*. Listen to the conversation and note the three main areas Claudia asks about.

1 _____   2 _____   3 _____

b ▶6.1 How do Claudia and Kevin focus on specific subjects? Complete the following phrases from the conversation using the words in the box. Listen again and check your answers.

> concerned   regard   regarding   regards   terms

1   ... *with* _____ *to the capacity,* ...
2   ... *in* _____ *of the number of people* ...
3   ... *as far as size is* _____ .
4   ... *And as* _____ *the graphics* ...
5   ... _____ *the schedule* ...

c Write questions using the following prompts and the phrases in Exercise 2b.

1   dimensions: what / overall size / module? With regard to the dimensions, what is the overall size of the module?
2   materials: what / bodywork / made of?
3   schedule: when / work start?
4   power: what / maximum output / need / be?
5   heat resistance: what sort / temperature / paint / need / withstand?
6   tolerance: what level / precision / you want us / work to?

3 a ▶6.2 Claudia goes on to ask about the physical effects the simulator needs to produce. Listen to the conversation and make notes on the following points.

1 Possible variation in simulator movement _____

2 Extent of physical effects required _____

3 Best way to assess physical effects _____

b ▶6.2 Listen again and explain what is meant by the words and phrases in bold.

1 ... *to what extent do you want the experience to be physical?*

2 *The degree to which it moves can be varied ...*

3 *... it's obviously difficult to quantify something like this ...*

4 *The only way to determine what's right is to actually sit in a simulator ...*

5 *... you can assess the possibilities.*

c Following the meeting, Claudia writes an email to update Rod, an engineering colleague. Read the extract and choose a word or phrase from Exercise 3b that means the same as the words in bold. Sometimes more than one answer is possible.

To: Rod Nelson
Subject: Mars Lander

In order to (1) **find out about** the simulator's dynamic capabilities, we looked at the types of effect the simulator should produce, and (2) **the amount** these physical effects should be felt by passengers. Specifically, the following issues were discussed:

- (3) **How severely** should the module generate vibration, to simulate engine thrust?

- How much buffeting should be simulated? That is, (4) **how severely** the module generates jolting, due to supposed atmospheric turbulence.

- (5) **How much** will passengers be exposed to constant linear G-force, to simulate deceleration?

In order to (6) **work out** the magnitude of the above parameters, it was decided that the prototype will be equipped with variable controls. This will enable the client to (7) **evaluate** different levels of severity through trials inside the simulator.

1 _____assess_____
2 _____
3 _____
4 _____
5 _____
6 _____
7 _____

4 You are consulting engineers preparing to work with a space agency to design an unmanned landing module. The module, which will carry scientific equipment, is intended to detach from a space ship orbiting Mars and land on the planet. At this stage, this is all you know about the project. In pairs, prepare a list of the main questions you will need to ask at the needs analysis meeting using the following ideas.

- type of scientific equipment
- size/weight of equipment
- solidity/fragility of equipment
- surface conditions at landing site

Suggesting ideas and solutions

5 **In pairs, discuss the following questions about creative thinking.**

- What are the most effective ways of coming up with ideas and finding ingenious solutions to technical problems?
- What do you think of brainstorming – generating lots of ideas randomly in a group session, without analysis initially, then subjecting each idea to analysis and criticism as a second phase?
- What do you think of evaluating ideas progressively – continually subjecting them to analysis and criticism?
- When creative thinking is required to solve problems, what are the pros and cons of working individually, in small groups, or in large groups?

6 a **Read the newspaper article and answer the following questions.**

1. How is the statue being made, and what is it being made from?
2. What is Rick Gilliam's role?
3. What will the statue be placed on in its final position in front of the museum?
4. What technical problem did they have to solve?

MAMMOTH PROBLEM BAFFLES ENGINEERS, SOLVED BY CAVEMEN

The new statue outside the Museum of Natural History has been a mammoth project, literally. The soon-to-be-completed sculpture portrays a life-sized woolly mammoth, carved from a single block of sandstone. Initially, one aspect of the project had engineers baffled. Rick Gilliam, the engineer overseeing the logistics, admitted that he and his colleagues had fried their brains trying to figure out how the 36-tonne monster could be lowered onto the stone plinth that will support it.

'We knew that we could put slings under the base of the statue, and pick it up with a crane,' he explained, and that transporting it from the stonemason's yard on a low-loader wouldn't be a problem. 'The problem is placing it on the flat plinth that supports it. How do you prevent the crane's slings from getting trapped between the base and the plinth, so that they can be withdrawn? We couldn't think of an easy way to do it.' The creative answer eventually came, not from the engineers, but from the stonemasons, who had affectionately been nicknamed the 'cavemen'.

b Rick is talking to Gabriella, an engineering colleague, about the problem of placing the statue. Before you listen, explain what is meant by the following terms and try to guess what the three possible solutions are.

> bar   drill   friction   a grab (on the end of a crane jib)
> horizontal   lifting eyes   resin   vertical

c ▶6.3 Listen to the conversation and summarise the ideas. How do their ideas compare with yours? Why is each suggestion rejected?

d Complete the following suggestions from the conversation using the words in the box.

> about   alternatively   another   could   couldn't   don't   ~~not~~

1   Why _____not_____ come up with a way of hooking onto the side of the statue?
2   Well, _____ we drill into it, horizontally …?
3   We _____ fill all the holes, couldn't we?
4   Or, _____ , we could make sure the holes were out of sight.
5   What _____ drilling into the top, vertically?
6   I suppose _____ option would be to use some sort of grab, on the end of the crane jib.
7   Why _____ we ask them?

e You are engineers working on the mammoth statue project, with the following technical requirements. In pairs, discuss possible solutions to the problem of placing the statue on the plinth using the phrases in the box.

> Alternatively   Another option would be …   Couldn't we …   We could …
> What about … ?   Why don't we … ?   Why not … ?

- No holes, slots or grooves may be cut in the statue. All of its surfaces must remain intact.
- No spacers may be left between the underside of the statue's flat base and the flat upper surface of the plinth. The two surfaces must be left in direct contact with each other.
- The statue must not be subjected to shocks. Sudden drops, even of a few millimetres, are out of the question, given the fragility of the sculpture, especially at its corners and edges, which can be damaged easily.
- Any accessory equipment may be used, within the limits of technical possibility and reasonable cost.

f The stonemasons suggested a solution to the statue problem. Read their idea on page 99 and compare it with your solution. What external factors could cause some problems with their idea? How could these be solved?

Assessing feasibility

8　**a**　In pairs, dscuss what is meant by *feasibility*.

b　Look at the flow chart and, in pairs, discuss how budgets and schedules affect the technical feasibility of design, development and manufacturing solutions.

Size of budget
A bigger/smaller budget often means …

Length of schedule
A longer/shorter schedule often means …

Technical feasibility
… more/less sophisticated/innovative design.
… higher/lower quality/reliability/efficiency.

9　**a**　▶6.4 Viktor, an engineer from a German company that makes and installs industrial gantry cranes, is phoning Rajesh, the construction manager of a manufacturing plant currently being built near New Delhi, India. They are discussing the gantry crane due to be installed at the plant. Listen to the conversation and answer the following questions.

1　Why are holes needed in the concrete walls?
2　What are *core drilled holes* and what are *preformed holes*?
3　In this context, what is meant by *play*?
4　What impact will the lack of play around the bolts have (on the construction)?
5　Apart from technical questions, what two issues will determine the most feasible way of forming the holes?

b　In pairs, compare core drilling and preforming with regard to the following feasibility issues. Which technique is most suitable for the situation in Exercise 9a?

> cost　precision　timescale

c　▶6.5 Viktor and Rajesh are assessing the most suitable method of forming the holes in the walls. Listen to the conversation and compare their answers with yours.

d　▶6.5 Listen again and answer the following questions.
1　What are the advantages of using preformed holes in terms of cost and timescale?
2　What's the main disadvantage of core drilling the holes?
3　What tolerance can easily be achieved with preformed holes?
4　What tolerance is required for the holes on this project?
5　What's the risk of using preformed holes?
6　What key feasibility issue does Rajesh identify?

e Complete the following expressions from the conversation using the words in the box and indicate the degree of feasibility each expression describes.

borderline ~~dead~~ forever leg painstaking peanuts perfectly stretching tall way

	☺	😐	☹
1 it'll be ___dead___ easy	✓	☐	☐
2 it'll cost _____	☐	☐	☐
3 it'll be quite a _____ job	☐	☐	☐
4 it's _____ feasible	☐	☐	☐
5 it's achievable, but it's _____ it	☐	☐	☐
6 there's no _____ you can do it	☐	☐	☐
7 it's _____	☐	☐	☐
8 it's a _____ order	☐	☐	☐
9 it'll take _____	☐	☐	☐
10 it'll cost an arm and a _____	☐	☐	☐

perfectly feasible	☺
feasible but challenging	😐
completely unfeasible	☹

f How feasible do you thing the following suggestions are? Label them ☺ 😐 or ☹ according to the key in Exercise 9e.

1 The machine parts are tricky to paint with brushes, or to spray. Why don't we dip them in paint?

2 The steel bar is 100mm in diameter. Couldn't it be cut by hand, using a hacksaw?

3 Silver's a good conductor. Why don't we use it for wiring, instead of copper?

4 Instead of putting lead ballast in the helium balloon basket, why don't we use water containers?

5 They've used the wrong type of fuel in the engine. I'd suggest stripping the whole thing down and cleaning it by hand.

6 They produce 6,000 units per day and normally do a quality check on 1% of them. Couldn't they check every single product?

g In pairs, give an appropriate response to the suggestions in Exercise 9f using the expressions in Exercise 9e.

10 In pairs, discuss the feasibility of the following solutions to the problem of forming accurately positioned holes through the plant walls in New Delhi. Student A, you are Viktor; Student B, you are Rajesh. Discuss technical issues, cost and timescale, and rank the solutions in order of feasibility.

1 Is a diamond drill really needed to go through reinforced concrete? Surely you can drill into concrete with an ordinary hammer-action drill? Wouldn't that reduce the cost?

2 Couldn't they make the preformed holes wider than required, so there's extra tolerance? Then, once the bolts are fixed, the space around them could be filled with cement.

3 Why not drill the holes in the steel beams on site, instead of pre-drilling them? Then they could be positioned to suit the location of the preformed holes in the wall. That way, it wouldn't matter if the holes in the walls were slightly out of position.

4 Instead of bolting through the concrete, what about adding extra steel columns that run down the walls? The beams could then be supported on these, and no holes would be required through the concrete.

Describing improvements and redesigns

11 Look at the slide from an engineers' training course, *Total Technical Improvement.* In pairs, suggest examples of technical improvements to illustrate each one. Are there other points that could be added to the list?

> **DEFINING IMPROVEMENT:**
>
> - BETTER-QUALITY MATERIALS
> - LOWER UNIT COST
> - MAKE LIFE EASIER FOR USER

12 a Look at the slide from a design meeting at a computer printer manufacturer. In pairs, suggest ways that the following printer factors might be improved in some of the areas on the list.

cables/connections   case   ink/toner cartridges   paper   power   software

> **Possible areas for improvement**
>
> 1 Aesthetics
> 2 User interface
> 3 Reliability
> 4 Consumables
> 5 Output quality and speed
> 6 Maintenance
> 7 Manufacturing
> 8 Environmental impact

b ▶6.6 Marta, a manager at the printer manufacturer, is briefing the design team on key requirements for the redesign of a printer. Listen to the start of the meeting. Which two areas on the slide in Exercise 12a are discussed?

c ▶6.6 Listen again and answer the following questions.
1 Should the layout and components of the new printer differ much from the existing design? Why (not)?
2 How many times has the existing model been improved in the past?
3 What consideration is behind the decision on how different the new software should be?
4 To what extent should the new software system differ from the existing one?

d Look at the following verbs from the discussion and find three examples where *re-* means *again*. Match the other three verbs to the definitions in the box.

improve overall   improve the details   stay (the same)

1 redesign *design again*
2 reinvent _____
3 refine _____
4 revamp _____
5 rethink _____
6 remain _____

e ▶6.6 **Complete the following expressions from the discussion using the words in the box. Listen and check your answers.**

> Achilles   back   drawing board   ground   heel   improvement
> leap   quantum   ~~reinvent~~   room   scratch   up   ~~wheel~~

1 _____reinvent_____ the _____wheel_____
2 *designing the whole thing from the* _____
3 _____ *for* _____
4 *the* _____
5 _____ *to the* _____
6 *make a* _____
7 *designing the system from* _____

f **Match the expressions (1–6) in Exercise 12e to the definitions (a–f).**

a waste time re-creating something that has already been created ___1___
b the biggest weakness _____
c start again because the first plan failed _____
d make huge progress _____
e design from the beginning _____ / _____
f potential for doing a better job _____

g **Rewrite the following sentences using the correct form of the expressions in Exercise 12e.**

1 Unfortunately, we had to scrap the concept and start again.
  _We had to go back to the drawing board._____

2 This problem is the product's most serious shortcoming.
  _____

3 There's no point redesigning what already works perfectly well.
  _____

4 It's a totally new design – we started from the very beginning.
  _____

5 The new design is so much better – it's a transformation.
  _____

6 I think there's definitely a possibility to do better in this area.
  _____

13 a **In pairs, discuss how computer pointing devices have improved since the first mouse was invented. Use the language from this section and the words in the box.**

> ball   buttons   first mechanical mouse   optical mouse   optical sensors
> refined mechanical mouse   sensitive surface   touchpad   wheel   wireless

b **You have been asked by a computer hardware manufacturer to think of some functional improvements and technical solutions for pointing devices. In pairs, discuss your ideas.**

c **Present your ideas in Exercise 13b to another pair.**

 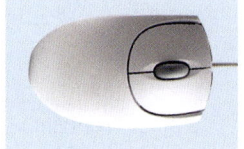  

- Describing health and safety precautions
- Emphasising the importance of precautions
- Discussing regulations and standards
- Working with written instructions and notices

Describing health and safety precautions

1 Some engineering or industrial activities are especially dangerous. In pairs, think of more examples to add to the following list.

- Manufacturing processes using dangerous chemicals
- Casting and welding involving high temperatures

2 a In pairs, discuss what is meant by the items on the Health and Safety meeting agenda.

b ▶7.1 Rosana, the assistant manager at a Dorian Food Processing plant, is chairing the weekly Health and Safety meeting. Listen to four extracts from the meeting and match each extract (a–d) to an agenda item (1–7).

a _____   c _____

b _____   d _____

Dorian Food Processing
Health & Safety Meeting Agenda

Wednesday 16 April, Conference Room, 2.00pm – 4.00pm

To: RM, MA, DB, SM, BP, LJ
Chair: Rosana Martinez

1   Hazardous substances & Personal Protective Equipment (PPE)
2   Harmful gases/fumes & asphyxiation hazards
3   Fire/Explosion hazards
4   Machinery: guards and safety devices
5   Access ways, guardrails and emergency exits
6   Electrical installations
7   Noise hazards

c ▶7.1 Listen again and match the words from the meeting (1–8) to the definitions (a–h).

1	confined spaces	a	burns the skin
2	CO_2 detector	b	contact (with a danger)
3	exposure	c	sources of ignition
4	irritant	d	small areas without ventilation
5	toxic	e	measures carbon dioxide
6	corrosive	f	poisonous
7	flammable	g	causes skin to react
8	naked flames/sparks	h	catches fire easily

d Which four types of PPE shown in the photos are mentioned at the meeting?

e In pairs, discuss the hazards in the following situations and the precautions that should be taken.

1 Working inside a container with limited air circulation
2 Cleaning metal using acid that can burn the skin and which gives off fumes
3 Using a grinder to cut through a steel plate
4 Applying paint that can cause painful rashes on the hands

3 a Stephanie, Dorian's senior safety officer, is attending a meeting on standard procedure for some engineering work that will be carried out at several of Dorian's plants around the world. Before the meeting she made notes. Read her notes and answer the following questions.

1 What is meant by *hazard analysis*?
2 What is another way to say *safe system of work*?
3 What type of work is going to be carried out, and where?
4 What is meant by *access to silos*?
5 What are the specific hazards relating to confined spaces in this situation?

> Hazard analysis & safe system of work
> Operation: Maintenance to grain silos involving welding (with oxy-acetylene)
> Location: Interiors of empty silos (approx 3m diameter x 15m deep), at bottoms
> Main safety issues: Access to silos for workers & equipment. Confined space hazards

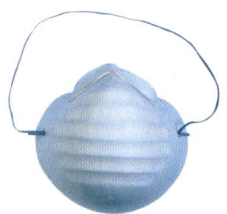

b ▶7.2 Stephanie is discussing some of the hazards with Ben, one of Dorian's engineering managers. Listen to the conversation and note the hazards that they mention.

1 Access hazards: _____
2 Confined space hazards: _____

c ▶7.2 Listen again and answer the following questions.

1 What safety precautions are discussed?
2 Which precaution might make one of the hazards worse, and how?

4 In pairs, discuss suitable health and safety precautions and PPE for the following operations on an existing steel petrol storage tank at a processing plant. Student A, you are a safety officer; Student B, you are an engineering manager. Use the phrases in the box. Swap roles and practise again.

- An opening needs to be cut through the wall.
- A new steel outlet pipe must then be welded onto the opening.
- The existing paint must then be removed from the external surface of the tank, by shot-blasting.
- The tank must then be repainted.

The main danger/hazard is …	They'll have to take care that …
Another danger/hazard is …	They'll have to be (very) careful …
There's a risk of … -ing	To be safe, they'll need to …

Emphasising the importance of precautions

5 a Dorian Food Processing is currently standardising safety procedures at its plants around the world. Read the following extract from the contents page of the company's new safety documentation and answer the following questions.

1 What is meant by LV and HV electrical maintenance operations?
2 What kinds of electrical maintenance might be carried out in a factory?

LV & HV ELECTRICAL MAINTENANCE OPERATIONS

Part 1 Identifying and designating Restricted Areas
(switchboards, transformer stations, areas with exposed conductors)

Part 2 Authorising maintenance
- The role of the Electrical Supervisor
- Procedures for issuing Permits to Work

Part 3 Isolating and energising circuits
- Lock-Out Procedure
- Temporary Warning Notices on switchboards

b ▶7.3 Listen to Stephanie explaining the safety procedures to Lin, the plant manager in Beijing. What is meant by the following phrases?

1 restricted areas
2 a permit to work
3 the electrical supervisor
4 the lock-out procedure

c ▶7.3 Complete the following extracts from the conversation by underlining the phrases that give the strongest emphasis. Listen to the conversation again and check your answers.

1 *Restricted areas are places where a serious danger is present. So it's essential that these should be kept locked **at all times / all the time**.*
2 ***Under no circumstances should anyone / Nobody should under any circumstances** be able to access them …*
3 *… it's important that permits are issued **each time / every single time** someone enters …*
4 *And it's crucial that there's **just one / just a single** key to each restricted area.*
5 *Then, while they're working, **it's vital / it's advisable** that they keep the key on them …*

d Which of the following phrases give more emphasis than *it's important*, and which give less?

1 it's crucial
2 it's essential
3 it's preferable
4 it's vital

e Rewrite the following precautions using the phrases in the box to add emphasis.

> ~~at all times~~   every single   it's crucial   it's essential   it's vital
> under no circumstances

1 The fire exit should always be kept clear.
   The fire exit should be kept clear at all times.

2 It's important to test that the circuit is isolated.
   _____

3 You should reset the alarm routinely when you start the system.
   _____

4 It's a good idea to check that the cable is not damaged.
   _____

5 It's recommended that you should only store non-flammable materials in this zone.
   _____

6 Nobody should enter the restricted area without permission.
   _____

7 Before pressurising the system, make sure all the connections are tight.
   _____

f In pairs, discuss the following basic precautions for working on electrical circuits.

Before starting:	During work:	To finish:
• Isolate circuit at switchboard	• Tighten connections fully	• Check no loose wires
• Test circuit – no current	• Don't damage insulation	• Test circuit

6 a Read the following extract from an electricity company newsletter. What procedure does the article describe?

> A helicopter hovers between the towering pylons of an extra-high-voltage power line. In a cradle, suspended several metres below the aircraft, stand two line men, shrouded in hooded, stainless-steel threaded hot suits. Just a few feet away is a live electric cable, fizzing with 400,000 volts. One of the men, holding a short metal wand, reaches out towards the cable. Pocket-sized lightning bolts arc through the air. There's no discernible electric shock, just a slight tingling sensation. A lead is then clipped to the live cable to maintain an electrical connection with the cradle and helicopter. The line men are now on, and maintenance work on the live power line can begin.

c In pairs, discuss the main precautions you think should be taken during live line maintenance work by helicopter with regard to the following hazards.

1 Collisions and snagging (getting caught/trapped)
2 Hazards from electrocution and heat
3 Mechanical failure (helicopter and equipment)

d ▶7.4 Krisztof, an electrical engineer, is describing live line maintenance by helicopter for a TV documentary. What precautions does he describe for each of the three types of hazard in Exercise 6c?

7 In pairs, think of an operation you are familiar with that requires safety precautions. Student A, you are a safety officer; explain the precautions to a new employee. Student B, you are a new employee. Swap roles and practise again.

Discussing regulations and standards

8 In pairs, discuss what is meant by *regulations* and *standards*, for example *safety regulations* and *design standards*. Give some examples of organisations and departments in your country and international bodies that produce these kinds of rules.

9 a Offshore oil platforms are covered by extensive safety regulations and design standards. In pairs, discuss the main hazards that oil platform workers face and suggest some safety precautions that need to be taken.

b ▶7.5 Isobel, a Health and Safety specialist, is speaking to newly recruited oil platform technicians on a training course. Listen to the introduction to her talk and answer the following questions.

1 What kinds of regulation will the course deal with?
2 What examples does the trainer give?
3 What important point is emphasised?

c Complete the following extract from Isobel's talk by underlining the correct words.

> *The focus of the course will be on your personal* (1) **legislation / <u>obligations</u>** *in terms of looking after your own safety, and the safety of others. That means we'll be focusing on specific safety regulations. For instance, we'll be looking at personal protective equipment that's* (2) **compulsory / prohibited**. *Or activities that are* (3) **compulsory / prohibited** *in certain areas, such as smoking. The majority of the obligations we'll deal with are legal* (4) **requirements / permits**. *In other words, they're* (5) **permitted / stipulated** *by law as part of health and safety* (6) **legislation / obligation**. *If you* (7) **contravene / comply with** *these kinds of regulations, it's not the same as turning up for work late, or merely breaching your contract of employment in some way. If someone fails to* (8) **contravene / comply with** *health and safety regs, they're breaking the law. It's as simple as that. I'm sure you're all aware of that, but it is an important point to emphasise.*

d Complete the following groups of synonyms using the words in bold in Exercise 9c.

1 illegal / banned / forbidden / *prohibited*
2 allowed / authorised / _____
3 adhere to / conform to / _____ _____
4 stated / _____
5 break (the law) / breach (regulations) / _____ (regulations)
6 laws / regulations / _____ / legal _____ / personal _____
7 obligatory / _____

10 **a** Read the extract from a guide to safety in the offshore oil industry. Complete the text using the words you wrote in Exercise 9d.

> The helicopter flights that ferry personnel to and from the platform are subject to specific safety (1) _legislation_. The procedures and standards that are (2) _____ by this regulations relate, principally, to the following areas:
>
> - Helicopter sea crash evacuation training. Courses are (3) _____ for all personnel
> - Design and safe operation of oil platform helidecks
> - Specialised pilot training.
>
> For North Sea oil platforms that fall within UK (4) _____ , operations must (5) _____ _____ the legal (6) _____ of British Health and Safety regulations, and Civil Aviation Authority rules. They must also satisfy the additional specific (7) _____ laid down by the UK Health and Safety Executive and the Offshore Industry Advisory Committee, Helicopter Liaison Group (OIAC-HLG).

b Read the following notes on the design requirements for helidecks on oil platforms. In pairs, discuss the possible reasons for these design standards.

> 1 Diameter of helideck: at least total length of largest helicopter
>   - no parts of aircraft overhanging perimeter
>
> 2 Approach/takeoff routes: adjacent structures below level of helideck - no tall structures
>
> 3 Perimeter protection (to prevent personnel from falling): handrail that can be lowered or horizontal net - no fixed handrails
>
> 4 Equipment to cope with bad weather / poor visibility: perimeter landing lights and anchor points

11 Imagine you are training new engineers in your workplace (or a workplace you know). In pairs, explain the main requirements of some regulations or standards that are relevant to your industry using the following points.

- key legal requirements
- the kinds of operation that must comply with regulations
- practices/procedures that are permitted
- practices/procedures that are prohibited

Working with written instructions and notices

12 Think of situations where written notices and instructions are used in industry. In pairs, discuss the following questions.

   1 What different kinds of information do they communicate?

   2 What are the characteristics of effective notices and instructions?

13 a The following warning notices are from a guillotine for sheet metal and a precision weighing device in a manufacturing plant. In pairs, discuss whether each notice warns of a problem that could injure workers, damage the machine, or both.

DANGER
Electrocution risk!
In event of fire use
CO2 extinguishers only.
Do not use water.

a

IMPORTANT
No user-serviceable
parts inside.
Opening panel
invalidates guarantee.

b

CAUTION
Lock guillotine
blade before
cleaning

c

BEWARE
Moisture-sensitive
device. Store in a
dry place.

d

WARNING
Take care when
lifting machine.
Hook crane to red
lifting eyes only.

e

b Look at the first word in each sign and answer the following questions.

   1 Which word is only used to warn of a risk of injury to people? _____

   2 Which word is only used to warn of a risk of damage to equipment? _____

14 a The following extracts are from the instruction manuals of three of the machines in Exercise 13a. In pairs, answer the questions (1–6).

a

In the event of a fire water extinguishers should not be used on this machine as it contains electrical circuits, and can therefore cause electrocution. Only a carbon dioxide extinguisher should be used.

   1 Why is it unsafe to put water on the machine?

   2 What type of fire extinguisher is recommended?

b

When lifting this machine, it is essential that only the two lifting eyes marked in red should be used. No other parts of the frame are load-bearing and must not, therefore, be used as anchor points.

   3 What is the purpose of the items marked in red on the machine?

   4 What could happen if the machine was lifted by other parts of the frame?

c

Care should be taken when cleaning below the guillotine blade as there is a danger that the blade may descend. Before cleaning, the control lever should always be set in the Blade Locked position. Protective gloves should be worn during cleaning as the sump below the blade may contain sharp metal off-cuts.

   5 Why is it important to lock the guillotine blade?

   6 What other danger is there, and what precaution should be taken as a result?

b ▶7.6 Petrus, an engineer from a machine manufacturer, is giving
instructions about the machines in Exercise 14a to a client. As you listen,
follow the written texts (a–c) and identify as many differences as you can
between the spoken instructions and the written instructions. Use the
following ideas.

1 grammatical differences
2 use of contractions
3 differences in words used

15 **a** Read the following spoken explanations of the operating precautions for an
industrial blower. Rephrase them as written instructions, making changes
based on the differences between spoken and written language style you
identified in Exercise 14b.

> You shouldn't place objects in front of the air inlet. And you should keep the inlet grille free
> from obstructions, and clean it regularly. If there's damage to the inlet grille, stop the blower
> immediately. Foreign bodies entering the duct can cause serious harm, because the unit
> contains precision-engineered parts revolving at speed, so it's highly susceptible to damage.

Objects should not be placed in front of the air inlet.
_____
_____
_____
_____
_____

> Before you start the blower, it's important to ensure that the external vents at the end of
> the air-intake duct are open. When you open the vents, fully extend the adjusting handle.
> Then when you close them, turn the handle and allow it to return under the force of the
> spring. Don't push the handle, because that can strain the spring mechanism, and result
> in damage.

Before starting the blower, ...
_____
_____
_____
_____
_____

b Think of some safety or operating precautions you are familiar with for a
machine or process you know. Write one or two paragraphs of instructions,
explaining the main precautions that should be taken.

c In pairs, explain the safety or operating precautions for the machine or
process using your instructions as a guide.

- Describing automated systems
- Referring to measurable parameters
- Discussing readings and trends
- Giving approximate figures

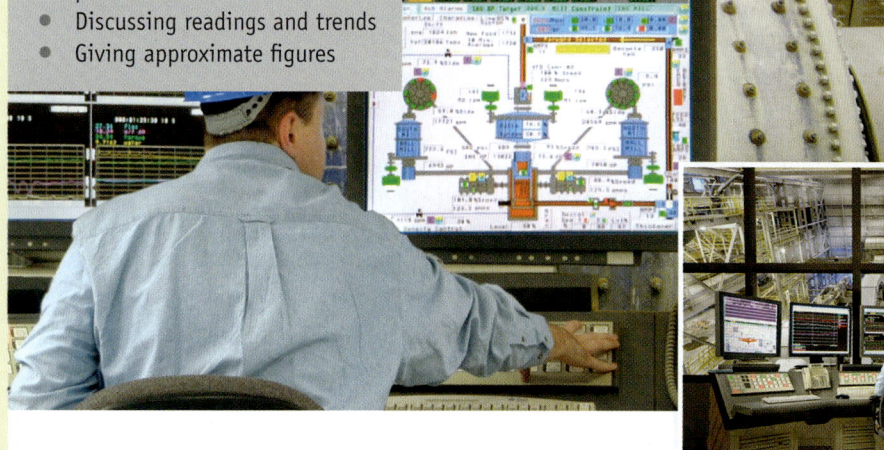

Describing automated systems

1 In pairs, discuss the difference between an automated and a manual system. What do you think a Building Management System (BMS) does in intelligent buildings? Suggest some operations that can be monitored and controlled automatically by the BMS in large buildings such as offices.

2 a ▶8.1 Roland, a mechanical and electrical services (M&E) engineer, is talking to Saskia, an architect, about the design of a new building. Listen to the conversation and answer the following questions.

1 What is a key characteristic of the client company?
2 How will this characteristic affect the building design?
3 What do you think is meant by *presence detectors*?
4 What does Roland say about design options and how does he describe option one?

b ▶8.2 Roland gives some examples of sensors and controls. Listen to the next part of the conversation and tick the points he mentions.

1 controlling the electric lighting inside the building ☐
2 controlling the amount of solar radiation entering the building ☐
3 controlling the air flowing in and out through the windows of the building ☐
4 controlling the flow of warm and cool air around the interior of the building ☐

c Match the words in the box to the synonyms (1–5).

detect ~~detector~~ pick up reading regulate set off trigger

1 sensor / _detector_
2 measurement / _____
3 control (adjust) / _____
4 sense / _____ / _____
5 activate / _____ / _____

d Complete the following extracts from the conversation by underlining the correct words.

1 *Not just the usual systems that __activate__/detect the lights …*
2 *We could use presence detectors to **pick up**/control other systems …*
3 *… a presence detector **sets off**/senses that everyone's left a meeting room …*
4 *… a temperature sensor picks up a positive **detector**/reading …*
5 *… the sensor **detects**/regulates sunlight, and **senses**/triggers the blinds …*
6 *… those sensors **set off**/sense a circulation system …*
7 *… we'd use presence detectors and heat sensors to **detect**/regulate as many systems as possible?*

e In pairs, describe the following automated systems using the words in Exercise 2d.

	sensor	parameter	system
1	presence detector	movement	lights
2	smoke detector	smoke	fire alarm
3	thermostat	room temperature	electric convector heater
4	pressure plate	weight of a person	intruder alarm

3 a ▶8.3 **Roland and Saskia go on to discuss an alternative control system in the building. Listen to the conversation and answer the following questions.**

1 What assumption is the idea based on?
2 What design approach might be taken with regard to controls?
3 What is the advantage of this approach?

b You are in the M&E design team for the new building project and have received the following email from the project engineer asking for your input. Read the email and, in pairs, discuss what the engineer wants you to do.

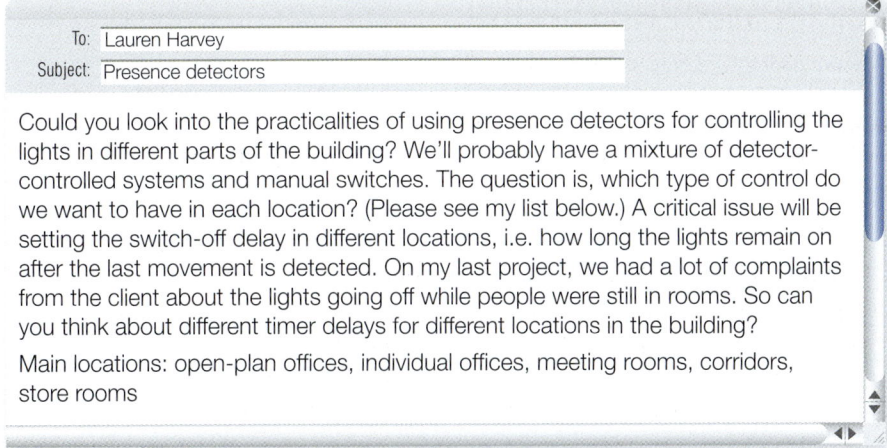

To: Lauren Harvey
Subject: Presence detectors

Could you look into the practicalities of using presence detectors for controlling the lights in different parts of the building? We'll probably have a mixture of detector-controlled systems and manual switches. The question is, which type of control do we want to have in each location? (Please see my list below.) A critical issue will be setting the switch-off delay in different locations, i.e. how long the lights remain on after the last movement is detected. On my last project, we had a lot of complaints from the client about the lights going off while people were still in rooms. So can you think about different timer delays for different locations in the building?

Main locations: open-plan offices, individual offices, meeting rooms, corridors, store rooms

c Prepare notes for a short talk to brief the project engineer using your ideas from Exercise 3b. Student A, you are an M&E engineer. Brief the project engineer on your ideas. Student B, you are the project engineer. Listen to the briefing and ask questions about specific details. Swap roles and practise again.

Referring to measurable parameters

4 **In pairs, think of monitoring and control systems that are widely used around the home. Discuss how the following parameters are measured and/or controlled in these common domestic appliances.**

Parameters: temperature   pressure   time   actions/movement
Appliances: boilers   heating systems   refrigerators   washing machines

5 **a** **Match the sensor or measuring system (1–5) to the industrial applications (a–e).**

1	pressure measurement	a	monitoring the speed of water travelling along a supply pipe
2	temperature measurement	b	measuring the level of heat generated by an exothermic reaction
3	flow measurement	c	monitoring the number of cans moving along a conveyor belt
4	level measurement	d	monitoring the amount of ethanol contained in a storage tank
5	process recorders	e	checking the force exerted by steam inside a vessel

b **In pairs, think of other uses for the kinds of sensor and measuring equipment in Exercise 5a.**

6 **a** ▶ 8.4 **Jochem and Katerina, two process engineers at a chemicals plant, are discussing the monitoring and control systems that will be needed for a new production line. Listen to three extracts from their discussion and answer the following questions.**

Extract 1   a   What problem is discussed?
                  b   What mechanical safety precaution is proposed?
Extract 2   c   What issue is discussed?
                  d   What three parameters related to consumption are important?
                  e   To calculate the parameters, what does consumption need to be continuously measured against?
Extract 3   f   What issue is discussed?
                  g   Which two measurements need to be taken?
                  h   What optimum value needs to be determined?

b **Match the words (1–10) from the discussion to the definitions (a–j).**

1	input	a	the best / the most effective/efficient
2	output	b	how often something happens
3	optimum	c	the amount of supplies/fuel used
4	differential	d	the total quantity so far
5	consumption	e	a specified period
6	cumulative	f	a value often expressed with per, for example units per hour
7	rate	g	the exit value, for example at the end of a process
8	cycle	h	the entry value, for example at the start of a process
9	frequency	i	the gap between two values
10	timescale	j	all the steps in a process, from start to finish

c The following specification was written following the conversation. Complete the text using the words in Exercise 6b.

> Vessel B1: Sensor and Measuring System Requirements
>
> Two pressure sensors: one located inside the vessel, and a second situated on the pipe running downstream, to enable any pressure (1) _differential_ to be detected.
>
> A flow meter to monitor gas (2) _____ . Data will be recorded as a (3) _____ figure (total usage), and as flow (4) _____ , in litres per second. Note: Software will be configured to log flow against the (5) _____ of a system clock, in order to pinpoint peak flow periods occurring between the start and finish of a given reaction (6) _____ , and to assess the (7) _____ with which they occur.
>
> Two temperature sensors: one at the entry point of the vessel, to measure (8) _____ temperature, and a second at the outlet point to monitor (9) _____ temperature. Note: Precise regulation of the entry temperature will be key to obtaining (10) _____ reaction performance.

7 a You and your partner are process engineers working with Jochem and Katerina at the chemical plant. You need to assess the sensors and measuring equipment required for the steam production facility. In pairs, discuss the requirements using the information in the diagram. Make notes of your ideas.

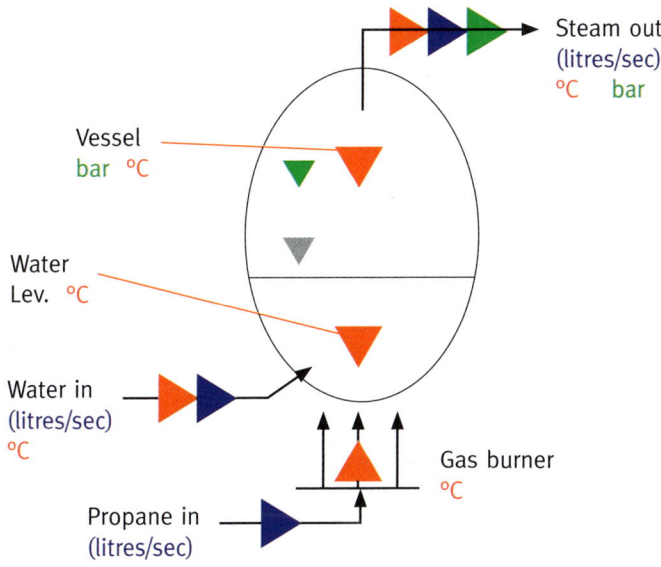

b In pairs, discuss what parameters can be determined for the installation of a heating cycle using your ideas from Exercise 7a. You should assume that all the measurements will be recorded against a timescale.

Discussing readings and trends

8 a In pairs, discuss the factors that cause mains electricity consumption to vary.

b ▶8.5 Helen, an electrical engineer at a power station, is giving a talk to a group of visiting investors. Listen to the talk and note the five factors that influence electricity consumption.

1 _____ 3 _____ 5 _____
2 _____ 4 _____

c Complete the following extracts from the talk using the correct form of the words in the box.

> decrease fall increase rise

1 *During periods of very cold or very hot weather, demand __increases__ .*
   The _____ in demand is obviously due to millions of electric radiators coming on …
2 *… a key factor which _____ or _____ demand, is whether or not it's light or dark …*
3 *… on cold, dark, winter evenings, the _____ in demand is significant …*
4 *Generally, demand _____ during the week, when factories and offices are operational …*
5 *So demand _____ at the weekend.*
6 *There can be a sudden _____ when people rush to switch kettles on, or heat up snacks in microwaves, and then a sudden _____ shortly afterwards.*

d ▶8.6 Listen to the next part of Helen's talk and answer the following questions.

1 Why does the company often have significant spare generating capacity?
2 What ideal situation does Helen describe?
3 Why is this ideal situation difficult to achieve?

e Match the words (1–8) from the talk to the definitions (a–h).

1	continuous	a	maximum power requirement at a given time
2	fluctuations	b	amount between an upper and lower limit
3	peaks and troughs	c	without interruption
4	peak demand	d	high points and low points on a graph curve
5	range	e	regular and repetitive
6	band of fluctuation	f	momentary rises followed by a fall
7	blips	g	changes, movements in general
8	continual	h	zone of up-and-down movement

f Look at the graph showing electricity demand fluctuations over a week in the UK. Find parts or patterns on the graph described by the words in Exercise 8e and analyse the fluctuations. How do they compare with Helen's explanation?

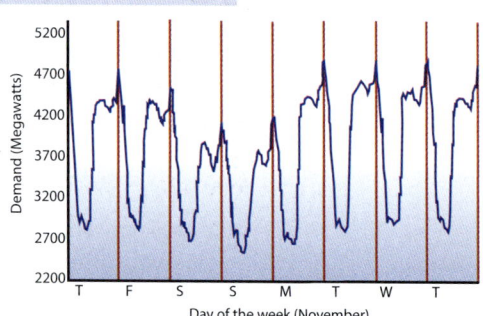

Day of the week (November)
Daily peak demand 8pm

9 **a** Read the document on energy saving aimed at industrial plant and facility managers. Complete the text using the words in Exercise 8e.

Dynamic demand control systems can be fitted to electrical appliances that operate on duty cycles, i.e. appliances that start up, run for a time, shut down again, and then remain on standby for a while before repeating the same cycle. Heating and refrigeration units are common examples of power-hungry equipment that operate on this start-run-stop-wait basis.

Dynamic systems exploit the fact that duty cycle appliances do not require (1) _continuous_ power. The purpose of the systems is to help smooth power demand for the benefit of electric utilities. To achieve this, they delay the start-up of the appliances they control during periods of (2) _____ . However, only minor adjustments are made to timing as, generally, the appliances concerned can only be held on standby for short periods as they need to run on a (3) _____ basis. But this still benefits electric utilities as it helps to avoid problematic, momentary (4) _____ on the demand curve.

Dynamic controls work by detecting slight (5) _____ in the frequency of the mains AC supply. Although this varies only within a very narrow (6) _____ , small drops in frequency indicate that power station turbines are working close to full capacity. The dynamic control system can therefore hold the appliance on standby for a short time until mains frequency increases again.

b Read the text again and answer the following questions.

1 What is meant by *duty cycle*?
2 What problem is dynamic control designed to avoid?
3 What sensor input do dynamic controls rely on to allow them to function?
4 What does the sensor input in (3) indicate with regard to power stations?
5 To what extent do dynamic systems modify duty cycles?

10 **a** Read the extract from the talk and, in pairs, discuss the following questions.

… electrical charge is extremely difficult to store in large amounts, you can't just charge up huge batteries. So we use an innovative technique to store up power potential during off-peak periods.

1 Why do you think this is such a major issue for power stations?
2 Can you suggest what innovative technique is used to solve the problem?

b ▶8.7 Helen goes on to describe the solution to the problem. Listen to the talk and make notes on pumped storage.

c Prepare a short talk on the operation of a pumped storage hydroelectric power station for visitors to the power generation company. Use your notes from Exercise 10b and the words in the box. Student A, you are an electrical engineer; Student B, you are a visitor on a tour of the plant. In pairs, give your talk and ask and answer questions. Swap roles and practise again.

| gravity | high level | low level | mountain | pumps | reservoir | turbines |

Giving approximate figures

11 **a** **Read the email extract and answer the following questions.**

1 Who do you think sent the email? What is their role within the company?
2 What type of review is the company going to undertake?
3 What is the objective of the review?

| To: | Gerry Klein |
| Subject: | Internal review |

Dear colleagues,

As you know, we are preparing to undertake a comprehensive internal review of the company's organisation and facilities. A key area of this review will be to assess how efficiently your engineering expertise is being utilised. I would emphasise that the aim of this assessment is not to question your professional competence. On the contrary, I and the company's new shareholders recognise the high degree of technical expertise within the organisation. Our intention is to work towards optimising this valuable resource by identifying the demands on your time that are largely unproductive (such as administrative tasks) in order to allow your skills to be used more productively.

b **The following extract is from a questionnaire used in the review which was sent to staff in the company's design department. Read the questionnaire and match each question (1–3) to points (a–c).**

Approximately what percentage of your time do you spend on the types of task below? For each question, the sum of values given for A + B should equal 100%.

1 A Doing technical tasks that use my engineering skills extensively _____ %
   B Doing moderately technical tasks that a less qualified colleague could do _____ %

2 A Doing technical tasks that add value (e.g. designing, problem-solving) _____ %
   B Doing tasks that do not add value (e.g. administration) _____ %

3 A Doing tasks that are purely technical _____ %
   B Doing tasks that relate to technical organization and decision-making _____ %

a The extent of technical role versus management role _____
b The degree of commercial exploitation of technical skills _____
c The degree of application of expertise and experience _____

c ▶ 8.8 **Eleanor and Gerry, two design engineers, are talking about the questionnaire. Listen and write approximate values, to the nearest 10%, for Gerry's answers to the questions.**

d **Complete the following sentences using the words or phrases in the box. Sometimes more than one answer is possible.**

ballpark figure   off the top of my head   nowhere near   pretty much
roughly   somewhere in the region of

1 They asked for a ballpark figure for setting up the new system.
2 I've got the figures in my computer, but I couldn't tell you _____ .
3 The work is _____ finished, there's just the tidying up to do.
4 The actual cost of the stadium was _____ the estimate at £2m over budget.
5 I think it'll take _____ two weeks to complete the report.
6 The development will cost _____ $10m.

e In pairs, ask and answer the questions from the questionnaire in Exercise 11b using the phrases in Exercise 11d. Note down your partner's answers.

1 A _____ % B _____ %
2 A _____ % B _____ %
3 A _____ % B _____ %

12 a ▶8.9 As part of the company's internal review, an assessment is being made of the hardware and software that make up the firm's Computer Aided Design (CAD) system. Dan, a design engineer, is talking to Beatrice, his manager, about the state of the system. Listen and mark the following statements True (T) or False (F).

1 Most of the screens are too small.
2 Engineers spend a lot of time working on screen.
3 Large numbers of drawings are printed at their office.

b Find words and phrases in audioscript 8.9 on page 93 to match the following definitions (1–5).

1 approximately / _____
2 much more than / _____
3 at least / _____ (two thirds)
4 most / _____
5 almost zero / _____

c Complete the following replies to express the figures in approximate terms using the words in Exercises 11d and 12b. Sometimes more than one answer is possible.

1 How old is this equipment? __A good__ five years old.   (at least 5 years)
2 What percentage of the PCs need changing? _____ all of them.   (95%)
3 How many of the computers are up to spec? _____ all of them.   (70%)
4 How many of the staff use the CAD system? _____ half of them.   (55%)
5 How much would the new printers cost? _____ $2,000.   ($3,120)
6 How much does an adapter like this cost? _____ .   ($2)
7 How long would a full system take to install? _____ 5 days.   (4–6 days)
8 Can most of our clients read these files? Yes, _____ of them.   (95%)

13 You are setting up a small company of consulting engineers employing seven members of staff – five engineers and two assistants. You need to rent an office, equip it with a computer network with CAD system and admin software, and buy other basic office equipment. In pairs, discuss some ballpark figures relating to the following questions.

● What computer equipment will be required and how much will it cost to buy?
● What other items of furniture/equipment will be needed, and how much will this cost?
● How much floor space will be required in the open-plan office?
● How long will it take to set up the office – install the furniture and equipment?

UNIT 9 Theory and practice

- Explaining tests and experiments
- Exchanging views on predictions and theories
- Comparing results with expectations
- Discussing causes and effects

Explaining tests and experiments

1 In pairs, discuss the following tests and experiments and their main advantages and disadvantages.

   1 computer models and simulations   2 reduced-scale testing   3 full-scale testing

2 a In pairs, suggest how the following development tools could be used for aerodynamic testing.

- Computational Fluid Dynamics (CFD)
- a wind tunnel equipped with a rolling road
- field testing

b ▶ 9.1 An international team of researchers are collaborating on the design of an experimental energy-efficient vehicle. They are discussing the tools available for developing the vehicle's aerodynamic design. Listen to the conversation and answer the following questions.

1. What options are available for wind tunnel testing in terms of scale?
2. Why are rolling roads useful in wind tunnels when testing vehicles?
3. What issue will determine whether or not a rolling road is necessary?
4. What point is made about the reliability of CFD and wind tunnel data?
5. What problem is mentioned with regard to outdoor testing?

c ▶ 9.1 Listen again and complete the following extracts from the conversation using the words and phrases in the box.

> The acid test   back-to-back testing   in the field   mock-up
> trial run   tried-and-tested   validate   ~~virtual~~

1. ... the tests would obviously be ___virtual___ , based on a computer model.
2. ... go into a wind tunnel, with a scale model, or a full-size _____ .
3. ... it's not just about data gathering. You also have to _____ the data.
4. The _____ only comes when you try out a full-scale prototype in real conditions. We need to make sure that everything is _____ outside, with a full-scale _____ .
5. ... with changeable weather, it's not easy to do _____ out _____ .

d Match the words and phrases in Exercise 2c to the definitions (a–h).

   a   a 3D model simulating shape and size, but without internal components
       ___mock-up___
   b   proven to be reliable through real use / trials _____
   c   outdoors, in a real situation _____
   d   describes something simulated by software, not physical _____
   e   a crucial trial to prove whether or not something works _____
   f   trials to compare two different solutions, in the same conditions _____
   g   prove theoretical concepts by testing them in reality _____
   h   a practical test of something new or unknown to discover its effectiveness
       _____

e Complete the aerodynamic design development plan of the energy-efficient vehicle using stages (a–e).

   a   Test model in wind tunnel to validate data from scale tests
   b   Carry out back-to-back tests in wind tunnel with mock-ups
   c   Build full-size working prototype
   d   Select best design, based on data from wind tunnel tests
   e   Narrow down design options to three, based on computer data

   Aerodynamic design development plan
   1   Experiment using CFD software
   2   _____
   3   Produce reduced-scale mock-ups of designs and test in wind tunnel
   4   _____
   5   Build first full-scale mock-up
   6   _____
   7   Produce two revised designs to improve on full-scale mock-up
   8   _____
   9   Select best design, based on data from tests
   10 _____
   11 Carry out field tests with trial runs outside

3 You are members of a technological research team similar to the one in Exercise 2b. You have been asked to design a test programme for an experimental system for air-dropping cargo. Read the brief and, in pairs, discuss the types of test required and their sequence.

Design brief

The system allows relatively fragile cargo to be air-dropped from planes into remote locations on the ground. It comprises a parachute, attached to a cylindrical container two metres long with a diameter of 1.5 metres. The container is surrounded by a deformable protective structure.

The aims of testing are to develop the designs of:

a) the parachute

b) the protective structure, in order to minimise the impact to cargo inside the container.

The number of tests must be maximised within a limited budget. As tests involving real drops from aircraft are costly, these must be kept to a minimum.

Exchanging views on predictions and theories

4 a In pairs, answer the following questions.

1   What kinds of cargo is sometimes dropped from aircraft, and why?

2   What are the advantages and disadvantages of air-drops?

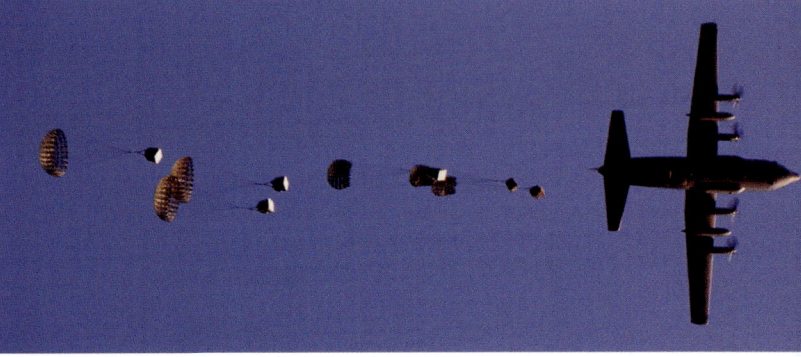

b Read the following predictions of how a container air-dropped with parachutes might behave while falling, and on hitting the ground. Complete the predictions by underlining the words you think are correct.

1   The longer the container is in the air, the more its horizontal speed will **decrease/increase**.

2   Compared with a low-altitude drop, the vertical speed of a high-altitude drop will be **lower/higher**.

3   In terms of damage to the container, a high **vertical/horizontal** impact speed is potentially worse.

4   A very low-altitude drop will most likely cause the container to **slide/roll** along the ground.

c ▶9.2 Arnaud and Jenna, two engineers, are talking at the start of an air-drop research project. Which predictions in Exercise 4b do they agree on, and which do they disagree on? How do their ideas compare with yours?

5 a Rephrase the words in brackets to complete the following extracts from the conversation.

1   *So,* _____ (in theory), *the horizontal speed will keep decreasing …*

2   *So,* _____ (assume) *the drop altitude's very low, …*

3   *…* _____ (sure) *a low vertical speed is the critical factor.*

4   *Because,* _____ (presume), *if the groundspeed's quite high, there's a danger the container will roll …*

5   *So,* _____ (argue), *rolling is the worst problem, …*

b Rephrase the words in bold in the following sentences using the words in Exercise 5a.

1   **I suppose** there'll always be a certain amount of groundspeed.

2   **If we assume** the container will roll, we'll need to protect it accordingly.

3   **According to the hypothesis**, groundspeed will almost always be positive.

4   **You could say that** it's inevitable the container will roll and bounce along.

5   **I'm convinced that** high vertical speed is less problematic than high groundspeed.

c   In pairs, decide whether the following words and phrases are used to agree or disagree. Can you think of other phrases for agreeing and disagreeing?

Absolutely   I'm not convinced   I'm not so sure   Not necessarily
Of course   True

d   Look at the diagram and, in pairs, discuss the following questions.

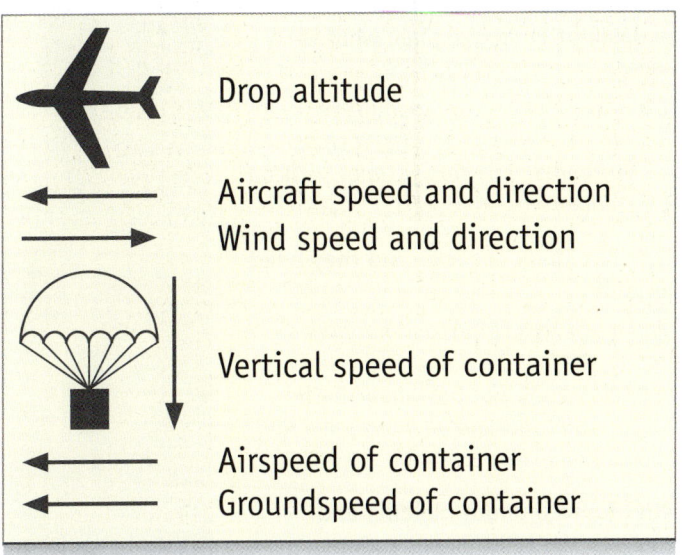

Drop altitude

Aircraft speed and direction
Wind speed and direction

Vertical speed of container

Airspeed of container
Groundspeed of container

1   What is the difference between airspeed and groundspeed? How do wind speed and wind direction result in a difference between an aircraft's airspeed and its groundspeed?
2   If an aircraft's groundspeed and airspeed are the same, what must the wind speed be?
3   In theory, an aircraft can fly with a groundspeed of zero in certain extreme conditions. What would these conditions be, with regard to wind speed and the aircraft's direction relative to the wind?
4   To minimise the horizontal groundspeed of an air-dropped container on landing, what should the aircraft's direction be, relative to the wind?
5   If several air-drops are carried out from the same altitude with different wind speeds, how will higher wind speeds affect the groundspeed of the container on landing?

6   a   In pairs, discuss which of the following options you think is preferable and why.

1   a low-level drop with low vertical speed and high horizontal speed
2   a high-level drop with high vertical speed and low horizontal speed

b   In pairs, discuss how the design of the container used for dropping cargo would be different for each of the two options in Exercise 6a. For each situation, consider how the container could be built to cushion the type of impact. In particular, think about the shape of the container and the protective structure around it.

Comparing results with expectations

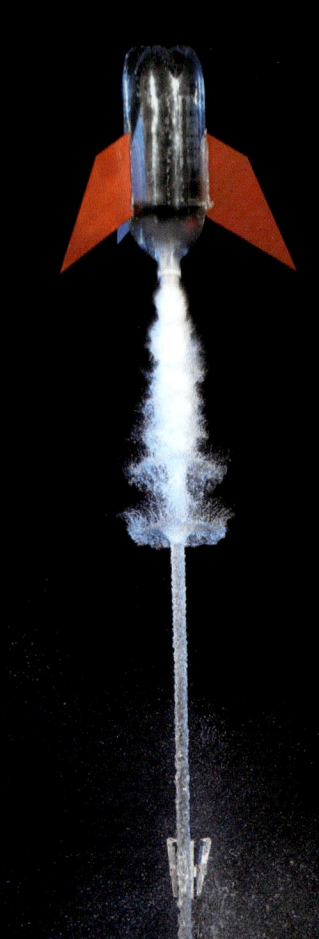

7 **a** In pairs, discuss the difference between expectations and results. Give an example relating to research and development (R&D) in engineering.

   b Manfred Haug, an aeronautical engineer, is describing his early rocket experiments. Read the description and explain what is meant by the expressions in bold.

*Relying on **trial and error** isn't always the best way to improve technology, but I found it was an effective way to develop rockets. Especially as rocket science was **unfamiliar territory** for me. I was on **a steep learning curve**, hence the numerous explosions.*

   c Read more of the description. What kinds of rocket did they build and how do you think they worked?

I should say that this had nothing to do with NASA, and happened a long way from Cape Canaveral. It was just me and a few friends on a windswept football field near Hamburg. But the plastic bottle water rockets we built and launched went through an impressive R&D programme, bearing in mind we were only 12 years old!

8 **a** ▶9.3 Listen to an interview with Manfred about building and launching water rockets and answer the following questions.

     1 How full were the bottles?
     2 What coincidence was helpful?
     3 How powerful was the rocket?
     4 What problem occurred?

   b Read the following extracts from the interview. What is meant by the words in bold?

     1 *… we **expected** it would shoot up reasonably fast …* _____
     2 *… we **didn't anticipate** just how powerful it would be.* _____
     3 ***It totally exceeded our expectations.*** _____

9 **a** In pairs, discuss two or three solutions to the problem experienced with the rocket, based on basic materials and simple assembly techniques. For each potential solution, explain how you would expect the rocket to perform and why, describing potential problems for each solution.

   b ▶9.4 Manfred goes on to describe how he and his friends solved the problem. Listen to the description and summarise the solution, explaining why it was effective. How does the solution compare with your ideas in Exercise 9a?

   c ▶9.4 Listen again and complete the following phrases from the description.

     1 (as expected)   *It didn't go exactly* _____ .
     2 (extremely well)   *It worked* _____ .

10 **a** In pairs, discuss possible ways of making the water rocket more powerful to allow it to attain higher altitudes. The basis of the design should be the same and you may only use basic materials. For each solution, explain the following points.

- Why you would expect the rocket to be more effective
- Any potential problems

b ▶9.5 Listen to Manfred describing how the rocket was developed and the results of further tests. Make notes on the improvements made and their consequences. How do the solutions compare with your ideas from Exercise 10a?

c Read the following phrases that Manfred uses. Complete the definitions by underlining the correct words.

1 *as it turned out* = what happened in **theory/**<u>**practice**</u>
2 *what actually happened* = what happened in **theory/practice**
3 *we underestimated the pressure* = it was **less/more** than we thought
4 *we overestimated the strength* = it was **less/more** than we thought
5 *plastic bottles are hardly up to the job* = they're **adequate/inadequate**
6 *I learned the hard way.* = it was a **theoretical/practical** lesson

d In pairs, discuss the following questions.

- Did you have any experiences of building things when you were younger which didn't turn out as you'd expected? What did you underestimate or overestimate? What lessons did you learn the hard way?
- When you were younger, what experiences were most beneficial in helping you to improve your technical skills? What technical principles did you learn?

11 Amateur rocket scientists have produced water rockets capable of reaching altitudes of several hundred metres in competitions. In pairs, think of initial ideas for a suitable design which complies with the following competition rules.

Water Rocket Competition

✵ Rockets must be assembled entirely from consumer products purchased from supermarkets or DIY stores. For safety reasons, no glass or metallic components are permitted.

✵ Rockets will be pressurised, and anchored during pressurisation using a compressor and launch pad provided by the organisers.

✵ Release of the rocket will be triggered by competitors, from a distance, by rope, at the moment deemed appropriate by the competitor, based on a reading on the pressure gauge of the compressor.

Discussing causes and effects

12 In pairs, discuss the difference between cause and effect in each of the following situations.

1 a vehicle tyre overheating
2 an electrical circuit overloading
3 a ship's hull corroding

13 a Read the title of the article in Exercise 13b and explain what you think it means.

b Read the article and answer the following questions.

1 What are chicken cannons designed to do?
2 Why was a chicken cannon used for a train test?
3 What were the effects of the test?

CHICKEN CANNON GOOF MAKES TECH EGGHEADS LOOK LIKE TURKEYS

When new aircraft are developed, jet engines and cockpit windshields are tested to simulate bird strikes (mid-air collisions with birds), which can result in damage. The tests are carried out using special compressed-air cannons that fire dead chickens. On one occasion such a gun was lent, by an aeronautical company, to some engineers developing a new train. Bird strikes were a potential danger, owing to the train's high speed. Having received instructions in how to use the cannon, the train designers bought an oven-ready chicken from a local supermarket, and subsequently fired it at their prototype.

The effects were devastating. As a result of the impact, a hole was smashed, not just through the windshield, but also through the back of the driver's compartment. It was hard to believe a chicken had caused so much destruction. Consequently, the engineers contacted their aeronautical colleagues to enquire if the problem might be due to an issue with the gun, some sort of fault that could have caused it to exceed its normal firing power. No malfunctions were found. However, it was later discovered that the unexpected damage had occurred because of a temperature issue.

---

c The text in Exercise 13b is an urban legend (or urban myth) – a commonly told story that is said to be true, but which is not. Can you guess what temperature issue caused the unexpected effects?

d Complete the following sentences using the words and phrases in the box.

because of (x2)   caused   consequently   due to   owing to   result in   result of

1 Bird strikes can ____result in____ damage to aircraft.
2 Bird strikes were a potential problem for the train, _____ /
_____ / _____ its speed.
3 During the test, the train was severely damaged as a _____ the impact.
4 The damage occurred _____ a problem relating to temperature.
5 The impact of the chicken _____ it to enter the train.
6 The engineers thought the gun was faulty, so _____ they called their colleagues.

e Read the following engineering urban legends and complete the descriptions of causes and effects using the correct form of the words and phrases in Exercise 13d. Sometimes more than one word or phrase is possible.

1 Apparently, the biggest challenge in space exploration was developing a pen for astronauts to use in orbit as ordinary ballpoint pens don't work in space, _because of / due to / owing to_ the fact that there's no gravity. So _____ this problem, there were teams of researchers working for years, trying to find a solution. Eventually, someone came up with the idea of using a pencil.

2 When they designed the foundations of the library on the university campus, they forgot to allow for the weight of the books on the shelves, which _____ the building to start sinking. So _____ , half of the floors have had to be left empty, without books, to keep the weight down.

3 Did you hear about that Olympic-sized swimming pool that was built? They got the length wrong, _____ the tiles. They forgot to take into account the thickness, which _____ the pool measuring a few millimetres too short. So _____ , it can't be used for swimming competitions.

14 a One popular topic for urban legends is the suggestion that the moon landings didn't really take place and were filmed on Earth. In pairs, discuss the following questions.

- In photos taken of astronauts on the moon, why are no stars visible in the sky?
- In film footage, why is the flag planted on the surface of the moon seen moving slightly?
- Why do photos of astronauts' footprints appear to be on a wet surface and not in dry dust?
- Why is no blast crater caused by engine thrust during the landing visible below the module?

b ▶9.6 Caroline and Renato, two colleagues at an engineering firm, are talking about the moon landings during a coffee break. Listen to the conversation and compare what they say with your ideas from Exercise 14a.

c In pairs, discuss any urban legends you have heard relating to engineering and technology. Use the following ideas to help you.

- unbelievable design faults
- bizarre incidents involving cars
- rumours about amazing experimental technology
- bad workmanship by builders, plumbers and electricians

UNIT 10 Pushing the boundaries

- Discussing performance and suitability
- Describing physical forces
- Discussing relative performance
- Describing capabilities and limitations

Discussing performance and suitability

1 a In pairs, answer the following questions about wind turbines.

1 What function do wind turbines perform?
2 What are the main advantages and disadvantages of wind turbines?
3 What types of location are most suitable for wind farms?

b In pairs, discuss the functions and technical characteristics of the following wind turbine components.

| blades   tower   generator |

2 a ▶10.1 **Mike, Loreta and Hanif, engineers at a wind turbine constructor, are discussing performance and suitability issues relating to offshore wind turbines. Listen to the conversation and answer the following questions.**

1 Which wind turbine component do the engineers discuss?
2 What is the big problem with offshore installations?
3 Which two types of construction material are being compared?
4 Why are coastal defences mentioned?
5 What point does Hanif make about regular maintenance?
6 What comparison needs to be made with regard to lifespan?

b Match the words (1–6) from the discussion to the definitions (a–f).

1	appropriate/suitable	a	the right solution for a particular situation
2	consistent/reliable	b	good enough for the intended function
3	cost-effective/economical	c	performs a function well
4	effective	d	works quickly and well
5	efficient	e	makes the most of resources, isn't wasteful
6	sufficient/adequate	f	doesn't break down, always performs in the same way

c Make the following words negative by adding the prefixes in- or un-.

1 adequate   *inadequate*   6 efficient   _____
2 appropriate   _____   7 reliable   _____
3 consistent   _____   8 sufficient   _____
4 economical   _____   9 suitable   _____
5 effective   _____

d ▶10.1 **Listen again. What issues do Mike, Loreta and Hanif agree and disagree on?**

3 **a** **The following information is from the web site of Sigma Power, a firm that advises corporate and government clients on wind energy projects. Complete the text using the words in Exercise 2c.**

Wind Turbines - FACT FILE

1	The fact that wind turbines consume no fuel and waste very little energy is clearly a fundamental advantage. But just how _efficient_ are they? Key figures
2	Clearly, wind turbines need to be located on relatively windy sites in order to function. From a meteorological standpoint, what kinds of geographical location are the most _____ ?
3	Turbines are generally placed at the tops of tall towers, where wind speeds are higher, thus making them more _____ . What other positioning factors influence performance?
4	Wind turbines rarely function continuously, due to the fact that wind speeds are _____ . How significant is the impact of variable weather conditions on power generating capacity?
5	Transmitting electricity over long distances is inherently _____ , due to power loss from overhead or underground power lines. Find out more about the advantages of generating power locally.
6	The generating capacity of wind turbines is generally _____ for it to be relied upon 100%. What percentage of total generating capacity can wind turbines realistically provide?
7	Some early wind turbines were _____ , suffering breakdowns caused by inaxial stresses stemming from higher wind loads on the upper blade. However, this problem has been overcome on modern units. Learn more about the technical evolution of wind turbines.

b **You are engineers at Sigma Power. The marketing manager has asked you to provide some technical answers for the frequently asked questions section of the company's website. The FAQ section is aimed primarily at potential clients who are thinking of installing wind turbines at their sites – factories, office complexes, hospitals, and university campuses. In pairs, discuss the following questions and write the answers for the website using the information in the fact file and your own knowledge.**

Frequently Asked Questions
A common-sense introduction to wind turbines

1	What's the big advantage of having a wind turbine at my site?
2	How dependable are wind turbines as a source of power, given that weather conditions are changeable?
3	What kinds of site are most suitable for wind turbines, relative to natural factors such as hills, the coast, and height above sea level?
4	What's the most appropriate location for my wind turbine, relative to local features on the site, such as trees and buildings?

Describing physical forces

4 a Read the following article. What is a solar tower and how does it use the
forces of expansion and pressure?

SOLAR TOWERS

The dawn of a new era in renewable energy?

The need to develop renewable energy is widely seen as a futuristic technological challenge. In reality, some of the most effective ways of harnessing horsepower from nature are based on concepts that have existed for donkey's years. The wind turbine is an obvious example. Another – less well known, but conceived almost a century ago – is the solar tower or solar chimney. And if the Australian company EnviroMission completes an ambitious solar tower project in the New South Wales desert, the technology could capture not just the sun's rays but the public's imagination worldwide. The firm is planning to construct a tower a colossal one kilometre high. If built, it will be the world's tallest structure by a huge margin.

How it works

A large glass enclosure is built, with a chimney at its centre. The sun heats the enclosure, causing expansion of the air inside. At the top of the chimney, the lower temperature and lower pressure due to the higher altitude create a pressure differential known as stack effect. This causes air to flow up the chimney. Electricity is generated by turbines at the bottom of the chimney, which are driven by the flow of air. The bigger the area of glass and the taller the chimney, the greater the airflow and the higher the generating capacity.

b What physical forces would act on a solar tower 1 km high?

c ▶ 10.2 Su, a structural engineer specialising in the design of very tall
structures, is giving a talk to a group of engineering students. Listen to the
talk. Which of the forces in the box doesn't she mention?

| bending   centrifugal force   compression   contraction   expansion |
| friction   pressure   shear   tension   torsion/torque |

d Label the diagrams using the forces in Exercise 4c.

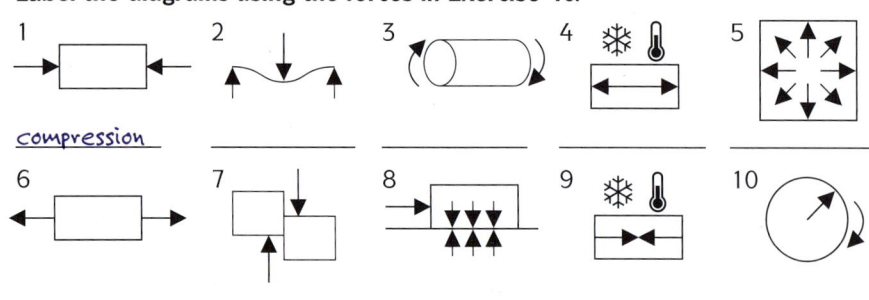

1 __compression__ 2 _____ 3 _____ 4 _____ 5 _____

6 _____ 7 _____ 8 _____ 9 _____ 10 _____

e ▶10.2 **Complete the following sentences from the talk using the forces in Exercise 4c. Listen again and check your answers.**

1 *So that downward force means the structure is in* <u>compression</u> *, especially near the bottom.*

2 *… a horizontal load, exerted by air _____ against one side of the structure.*

3 *Because the structure is fixed at ground level, and free at the top, that generates _____ forces.*

4 *… when elements bend, you have opposing forces: _____ at one side, _____ at the other.*

5 *… the wind effectively tries to slide the structure along the ground, and the foundations below the ground resist that. The result of that is _____ force …*

6 *… the foundations need to rely on _____ with the ground to resist the pull-out force, …*

7 *The action of the wind can also generate _____ . You get a twisting force …*

8 *When concrete absorbs heat from the sun, you get _____ ; as soon as the sun goes in, there's _____ .*

f You and your partner specialise in designing structures for electrical transmission grids. You are currently working on a cable support concept for power lines near wind farms exposed to severe weather. You have come up with the following design. In pairs, hold a short meeting to evaluate your design concept. Explain the forces acting on the structure.

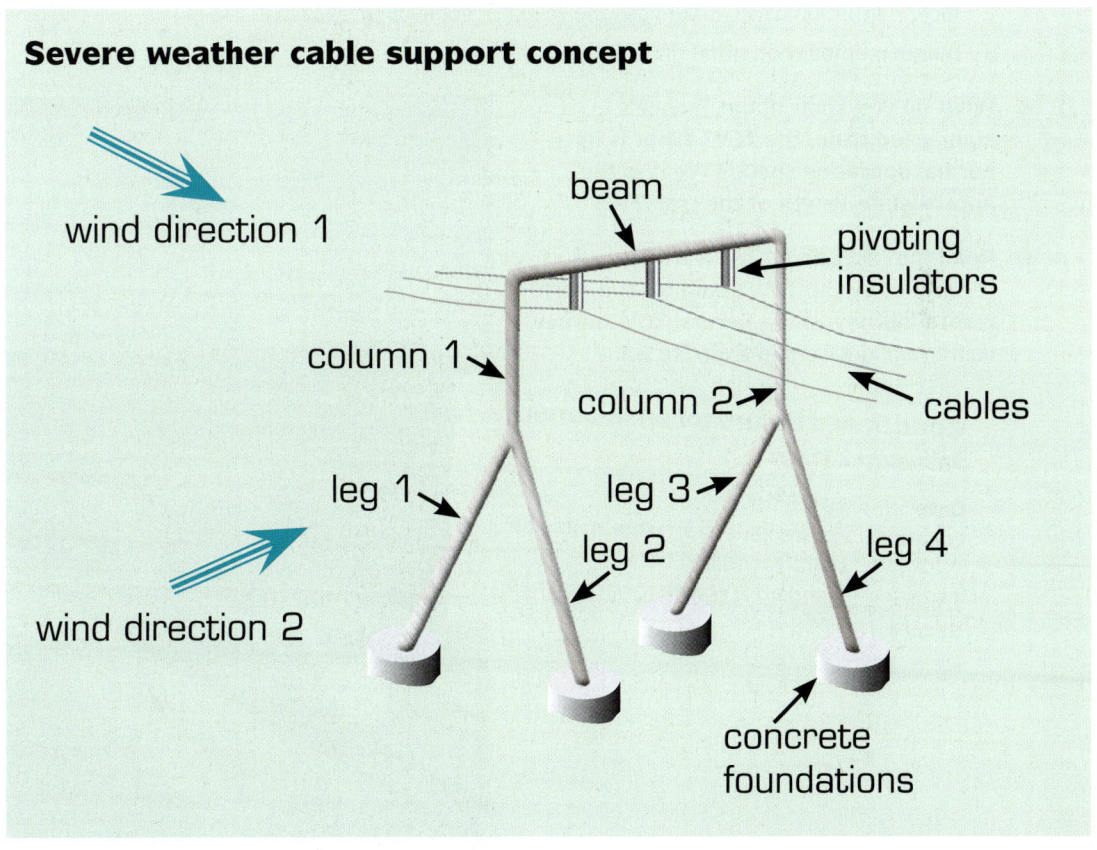

Severe weather cable support concept

wind direction 1

beam

pivoting insulators

column 1

column 2

cables

leg 1

leg 3

leg 2

leg 4

wind direction 2

concrete foundations

Discussing relative performance

5 a In pairs, discuss the advantages and disadvantages of air and high-speed rail travel. Focus on trips of between 500km and 1,500km, the journey length over which planes and trains often compete for the same passengers.

b Read the extract from an article about transport in a popular science and technology magazine and answer the following questions.

   1 What factors should be considered in the comparative analysis described?
   2 What is the purpose of the comparative analysis?
   3 What suggestion is made about Europe?

> Speed, convenience, efficiency, and environmental-friendliness: four factors with which to assess the relative effectiveness of different long-distance, mass-transport solutions for passengers. Technology: the key criterion in determining what transport solutions are available. And distance: the main consideration when categorising routes. Blend these variables together in varying quantities, and you have a model for calculating the optimum way of moving people.
>
> On a European scale, whichever way you mix the various criteria, the most advantageous way of getting people around the heart of the continent seems to be on high-speed, electric trains.

c Find words in the text in Exercise 5b to match to the following definitions. Which one of the words has a plural form?

   1 standard by which you judge something _____
   2 fact or situation which influences the result of something _____
   3 number, amount or situation which can change _____

6 a What do you know about France's high-speed train, the TGV? What is its normal operating speed? What is the approximate length of the train?

b Read the facts about the world speed record set by the TGV. Compare the world record journey with a normal TGV journey, using your answers in Exercise 6a.

World Speed Record for an In-Service Passenger Train

Date	April 3, 2007
Location	France: Paris to Strasbourg line on slightly modified track
Train	Standard TGV with fewer coaches
Record	574.8 km/h

c ▶10.3 Andrej, a consulting engineer specialising in rail technology, is talking about the TGV world speed record. Listen to the talk and answer the following questions.

1 Overall, how heavily modified was the train?
2 How long was the record-breaking TGV?
3 Why was some of the bodywork modified?
4 Why was the diameter of the wheels changed?

d ▶10.3 Listen again and complete the following table about the modified TGV using the figures in the box.

+ 68%   + 19%   − 15%   − 50%   + 80%

Technical criteria	Modified TGV: % difference from standard model
Maximum speed	
Train length (with coaches)	
Aerodynamic drag	
Diameter of wheels	
Motor power output	

e Complete the following sentences from the talk by underlining the correct words.

1 *The record speed exceeded the standard operating speed by a **tiny**/**huge** margin.*
2 *The train was modified to a **certain**/**considerable** extent …*
3 *… the modified train was **significantly**/**slightly** shorter, …*
4 *… changes were made to the bodywork, to make it **slightly**/**much** more aerodynamic …*
5 *The wheels on the modified train were **marginally**/**substantially** bigger …*
6 *… the power of the electric motors was **marginally**/**substantially** higher than the standard units …*
7 *… standard high-speed trains can be made to go faster by a **slight**/**considerable** amount.*

f Rewrite the following sentences to describe the modifications that were made to the TGV for the record attempt. Use the phrases in Exercise 6e to replace the words in bold.

1 The supply voltage in the catenary cables had to be increased **from 25,000 to 31,000 volts**.
2 To limit oscillation, the tension of the catenary cables had to be increased **by 60%**.
3 On some curves, the camber of the track had to be increased **by a few centimetres**.
4 The 574.8km/h record beat the previous record, set in 1990, **by 59.5 km/h**.
5 In perfect conditions the TGV could probably have gone faster **by 5 to 10 km/h**.

7 In pairs, choose a product or type of technology you know well and compare its performance and quality with an earlier model, describing the extent of the differences.

Describing capabilities and limitations

8 a **Look at the photos and read the extracts from *The Story of John Paul Stapp*, by Nick T. Spark, and answer the following questions.**

1 When and where do you think it took place?
2 What do you think the aim of the test was?
3 What do you think John Stapp's profession was?
4 What equipment do you think was used?
5 What do you think happened in the experiment?

> With five seconds to go Stapp activated the sled's movie cameras, and prepared for the shock. *Sonic Wind*'s nine rockets detonated with a terrific roar, sending out trails of fire and blasting Stapp down the track.

> … *Sonic Wind* hit the water brake. The rear of the sled tore away. The front continued, hardly slowing at all until it hit the second water brake. Then, spray exploded from the back of *Sonic Wind*. It stopped like it had hit a concrete wall.

b ▶10.4 **Listen to an extract from a documentary about the experiment and check your answers to Exercise 8a.**

c **Complete the following data on the *Sonic Wind* test using the figures in the box.**

> 1.2   3   20   46   1015

1 Max speed: _____ km/h
2 Acceleration from 0 to max speed: _____ seconds
3 Acceleration force: _____ Gs
4 Deceleration time: _____ seconds
5 Deceleration force: _____ Gs

d ▶10.5 **Listen to the next part of the documentary and check your answers to Exercise 8c.**

e **Complete the following groups of synonyms using the words in the box.**

> able to   capable of   cope with   exceed   incapable of
> intended for   ~~subjected to~~   surpass   unable to   withstand

1 exposed to (a force) / *subjected to*
2 resist (a force) / _____ / _____
3 go beyond (a limit) / _____ / _____
4 suitable for (a use) / _____
5 can / _____ / _____
6 can't / _____ / _____

f Complete the following sentences about *Sonic Wind* using the correct form of the words in Exercise 8e.

1 The bolts fixing the camera to the sled had to _cope with_ high shear forces.
2 The sled's rockets were _____ generating enormous thrust.
3 The pools at the end of the track were _____ stop the sled rapidly.
4 The skids on the sled had to _____ high levels of friction.
5 At full speed, John Stapp was _____ several tonnes of air pressure.
6 The rear of the sled was _____ resist the shock of deceleration, and broke off.
7 Doctors thought people were _____ surviving forces of 17 Gs and above.
8 John Stapp _____ the 17 G limit by a huge margin.

9 a You are a consultant engineer and your firm have received an email from an entrepreneur with an ambitious plan. Read the following email extract and note the key information.

b In pairs, discuss the key information in Exercise 9a and consider the following points.

- the level of G force
- a safe length for the track
- the feasibility of using wheels
- the suitability of the braking systems suggested

c ▶ 10.6 Jasmine and Andrew, consulting engineers, are discussing the issues in Exercise 9b. Listen and compare what they say with your ideas from Exercise 9b.

d In pairs, discuss the points raised in their conversation and make notes summarising your thoughts in preparation for a meeting with the entrepreneur.

e Prepare a short presentation for the entrepreneur using your notes from Exercise 9d. Student A, you are the consultant engineer. Give the presentation. Student B, you are the entrepreneur. Listen and ask questions about specific details. Swap roles and practise again.

To: Jasmine Murray

Subject: Rocket sled ride

The proposal is to build a rocket sled ride on a desert site in Western Australia. The ride will be aimed at wealthy tourists, and will allow them to experience supersonic speeds. We envisage carrying two passengers at a time, seated behind the pilot. The idea is inspired by the Sonic Wind experiments, which I'm sure you're familiar with. However, it goes without saying that safety will be the number one priority, which means that extremes of acceleration and deceleration must be avoided. For instance, a water brake, like the one used in the Sonic Wind tests, is clearly out of the question.

The site is large enough to accommodate a track up to 16 km long, though I reckon 10 km would be adequate. According to my rough calculations, that would be sufficient to allow progressive acceleration up to and through the sound barrier to about 350 m/s, and progressive deceleration to a standstill without exceeding 2 G (20 m/s²), while still leaving three to four kilometres of track as a safety margin. However, I'm not an engineer, so would appreciate your professional opinion on that.

In terms of basic technology, I assume the most suitable vehicle would be a rail-mounted sled, with steel skids that grip the track, above and below the rails, to prevent derailing, and avoid problems with aerodynamic lift. I assume wheels wouldn't be feasible given the speeds involved, though I'm not 100% sure about that. Perhaps you can advise. Propulsion would be provided by a rocket or aircraft jet. I already have a consultant sourcing a suitable engine, however, so that angle is being looked into.

As far as your input is concerned, the main area where I need your expertise is on the braking system. As I said, violent braking is out of the question. As I see it, suitably gentle options include systems that apply friction to the rails, aerodynamic flaps, parachutes, or reversed engine thrust. But, again, I'm not an engineer, so I look forward to discussing your thoughts on these issues.

AUDIOSCRIPT

1.1

Paula: Obviously navigation is the primary application of most GPS devices.

José: Sure.

Paula: Then you've got associated applications, uses that are related to navigating, such as tracking systems you can use for monitoring delivery vehicles and finding stolen cars, that kind of thing.

José: Mm.

Paula: And then there are more creative features. A good example would be on a boat GPS, you get drift alarms. So if the anchor starts to drag and the boat starts moving, there's a setting on the GPS that allows it to detect the movement, and an alarm sounds to warn you, and prevents the boat from drifting unnoticed.

José: I see.

Paula: Or another example on boat systems is man overboard buttons. So if you're sailing along and someone falls into the sea, you hit a button, which logs the position and ensures that you don't lose track of where you were, which then enables you to turn round and come back to the same point and find the person.

José: Right.

Paula: So, these are the kinds of applications we want to develop, more specialised, and more creative.

José: So, effectively, you're not talking about technical innovations. What you're really looking for is innovative ways of actually using the technology.

Paula: Precisely. Because these days, from the end-user's point of view, accuracy is no longer the main selling point. Most devices are accurate enough. The key is to make them more useful. So in terms of development, that's the kind of …

1.2

James: The engineering challenge of connecting a satellite to earth using a cable is, obviously, significant. In order to support its own weight, and be securely attached at each end, the cable would require a phenomenal strength-to-weight ratio. Carbon nanotube materials might, one day, be up to the job. And I'll talk about those in detail later on. How could vehicles be raised into space, up the cable? Well, using a self-contained energy source would be problematic, due to the weight of fuel or batteries required to power the vehicle. There are two possible ways round this problem: transmitting electricity wirelessly, or using solar power. The first technique is only in the early stages of research. The second would allow the vehicle to ascend only very slowly, though this wouldn't necessarily be a problem, as the car could be controlled remotely, allowing it to transport payloads as an unmanned vehicle.

1.3

James: The offshore base station would be supported by a floating structure, which could be attached to the seabed by anchors. Payloads could be carried from the shore to the station by ship before being lifted into orbit. The main advantage of a floating mobile station, rather than a fixed base on land, would be to help reduce the risk of a collision between the cable and one of the many lumps of space debris, such as redundant satellites, that litter orbital space. Based on careful monitoring of debris movements, in the case of an alert the station's anchors could be raised and the station could be moved, driven by propellers, to a new location out of harm's way.

1.4

1

Stefan: So, as you can see from this cross-section, we've come up with a completely unique profile. It's exclusive to this company and unlike anything else on the market.

2

Stefan: One of the key advantages of this new form is that it dramatically reduces vibration, which was always a problem before. Obviously, machines like these can never be entirely free from vibration but the new design runs extremely smoothly.

3

Stefan: Another advantage of the new profile is that it's considerably lighter, due to the reduced area of the overall section. So compared with our previous range, it's highly efficient, especially in applications that require continual starting and stopping, where low inertia is important.

4

Stefan: We're still conducting long-term reliability tests, but trials so far suggest the design is exceptionally durable, primarily as a result of the low vibration levels. We expect it to be significantly more reliable than rival units that are on the market, which is obviously an important selling point.

1.5

Richard: If you're talking to non-specialists, and you start using jargon, then to your audience, it's just going to sound like nonsense. That's one problem. Another relates not so much to language, but to the complexity of the technology you're talking about. Even if you use everyday language, the engineering concept itself might still be difficult to explain. And that can make the subject very heavy going, and quite dull, which is obviously not what you want. However, I think it's important not to oversimplify things. There's nothing worse than being spoken to as if you're a child. You don't want to sound patronising.

1.6

Richard: It's obviously best to use everyday language as far as possible. But I don't think that means avoiding jargon altogether. I find the best approach, so as not to sound patronising, is to use a certain amount of technical language, and then immediately afterwards give straightforward explanations of what it means using everyday words. When it comes to explaining tricky technical concepts, a good technique is to make comparisons between the technical point you're trying to illustrate and things from everyday life that people are familiar with, to help them paint a picture in their minds. There's then to help lighten things up, and stop things from sounding dull, I think it's good to use a bit of humour as well, and maybe a few amusing anecdotes.

1.7

Richard: As you can see, we've started work on the substructure, in other words the part of the structure that's below ground level. The foundations are concrete piles. Basically, a pile is a column going down into the ground. And we're using what we call bored in situ concrete, in other words, we bore, or drill, a hole in the ground, and concrete's poured in in situ, which means it's actually poured on the construction site, in its final position. An alternative is to use what we refer to as pre-cast driven piles. Pre-cast refers to the fact that the piles are made at a factory away from the site, before being delivered. They're then driven into the ground. They're hammered in with a pile driver which, put simply, is just like a giant hammer. And they don't just drive in piles, they drive everyone mad with the constant boom-boom-boom all day long. So, thankfully for our ears, we're not using that technique. Instead, we're boring the piles. The pile auger over there is effectively just like a giant drill. As it drills into the ground, we pump a special liquid called bentonite into the hole. Essentially, it's a kind of clay suspension, a sort of mud. And that prevents the walls of the hole from collapsing inwards. So when the hole's finished, it's full of bentonite. It looks just like a big muddy puddle on the ground. Obviously, it's not a good idea to step in one, like a colleague of mine once did, and then had to drive home in his underpants for a change of clothes. So, once the hole's been bored and filled with bentonite, they lower in some steel reinforcement. And then concrete's pumped in. And because the concrete is denser than the bentonite, it displaces it. So, in simple terms, if you picture a glass full of water and imagine pouring concrete into the glass, the water would overflow, and you'd end up with a glass full of concrete. So, that's piling. If anyone has any questions, by the way, just …

2.1

Irina: The only way to assess the environmental impact of a given material properly is to carry out an environmental audit and analyse the total impact of that material on the environment. I emphasise *total impact* because it's all too easy to judge materials and products on single aspects of their ecological impact. As an example, if we compare traditional and energy-saving light bulbs it's tempting to say energy-saving ones are better because they consume less energy. In fact, that's just part of the picture. That's just the *in-use* phase. You also need to consider the *pre-use* phase – in other words, the environmental impact of mining the materials used to make the bulbs, of transporting those materials to the factory, of manufacturing them etcetera. Then there's the *post-use* phase. How easy is it to recycle spent bulbs? And when you start to consider all of these factors, suddenly the comparison between classic bulbs and their energy-saving equivalents becomes much less clear-cut. Some of the materials used in energy-saving lights are problematic from an environmental standpoint, both in terms of acquiring them and recycling them. So the point is, it's essential to look at the whole picture. And doing that can be quite a complex task, as we'll see later on.

2.2

Sophia: OK, so steel bodywork versus aluminium bodywork.

Pete: What about pre-use, then?

Sophia: Well, I think it takes a lot of energy to produce aluminium, compared with steel, because aluminium's made by electrolysis.

Pete: Yeah. So steel's better, presumably.

Sophia: I think so, yeah. But, hang on a minute, with aluminium, it depends how much is derived from ore, and how much Is recovered from recycled material. As far as I know, recycling aluminium takes less energy. So I'm not really sure.

Pete: Presumably, it'll be mixed, won't it? For a given batch, there'll be so much new material, and so much recycled material.

Sophia: Probably, yeah. OK, so that needs to be researched, then.

Pete: Is car bodywork galvanised when it's made from steel?

Sophia: Um … good question. I'm not sure.

Pete: If it is, if it has to be coated with zinc, then that would take extra material and extra energy. So that's an important consideration.

Sophia: Mm, true. OK, so that's another question to note.

Pete: Then there's the energy consumed when they're transporting bulk metal to the car plant.

Sophia: Presumably aluminium takes less energy to transport, being lighter.

Pete: I'd say so, yeah.

Sophia: OK. What about manufacturing?

Pete: Well, aluminium would be lighter to handle, wouldn't it? It probably takes less energy to cut, as well.

Sophia: Yeah. Not sure whether it takes less energy to weld, compared with steel.

Pete: Good question. Another thing to check out.

Sophia: Mm, what about in-use, then? I assume aluminium's better because it's lighter, so you consume less fuel.

Pete: Yeah. And it should last longer, as well.

Sophia: Mm, is that an environmental consideration, though?

Pete: Well, yeah, because if things last longer, they need to be manufactured less often. So you use less energy.

Sophia: True. But then, is the lifespan of a car determined by the life of its bodywork?

Pete: Ah. Good point.

Sophia: It's usually determined by the chassis, or the engine, isn't it?

Pete: Is it?

Sophia: Mm, another one to be researched.

Pete: OK, what about post-use, then?

2.3

Margit: So, in terms of the main components, the conductor, at the centre, is copper or aluminium, depending on the model. That's then coated with polyethylene insulation and surrounded by steel wire, which provides the armoured protection. As the steel obviously needs to be protected from moisture, there's a plastic waterproof membrane around that. Then, the whole thing's surrounded by an outer jacket which, again, is in plastic-based material.

2.4

Toby: That's certainly a scary-looking collection of tools.

Esther: Yes, some of them do look quite menacing, don't they?

Toby: Is that titanium? The drill handle?

Esther: Um … yes.

Toby: I'm an engineer, that's why I, um …

Esther: Oh, I see. Yes, titanium's great. It's expensive, obviously, but very light. That's the big advantage. Ideally, you want it to be lightweight, to give you better control.

Toby: Nn.

Esther: These are the most impressive things, though, the burs on the end. The latest ones can rotate at over half a million revs per minute.

Toby: Nn.

Esther: They're coated with tungsten carbide, which I think is one of the hardest materials in existence, isn't it? Along with diamond. That's also used.

Toby: Nn.

Esther: The key requirement is abrasion resistance, of course. Obviously, they need to be very durable. And you don't want them snapping, either. The last thing you want is a brittle material. Apparently, that was the trouble they had in the past, making the bur tough enough so it didn't break. I think part of the problem was heat, as well. Drilling into a tooth at high speed, you obviously get a lot of heat build-up. You need a good degree of thermal stability.

Toby: Nn.

Esther: See what I mean? You can actually smell burning. And that's after a few seconds. Imagine the heat build-up after several minutes.

Toby: Nn.

2.5

Tom: Speaking as an engineer, Louisa, my view is that all the materials we use should be genuinely suitable for making watches, and not just chosen as marketing gimmicks. We're often guilty, in my view, of using exotic-sounding materials that are not particularly suitable from a technical standpoint.

Louisa: Yeah, I know what you mean.

Tom: A good example was that debate we had on whether to use submarine-grade steel in some models, to give the impression that they're exceptionally resistant to water. OK, submarine steel's good at withstanding the pressure of being a mile beneath the sea. But it's heavy. If it's not coated, its corrosion resistance is not that good, at least compared with other metals like titanium. It's also fairly poor in terms of looks, in my view. Water resistance isn't a question of metal quality, it's about the quality of the joints and seals you use. So, as a watch material, for me, it's not at all suitable. Tremendously marketable, I'm sure, but …

Louisa: Hm. No, I take your point. But I think it's fair to say that we've never chosen a material for marketing reasons that's insufficiently durable or not adequately built in any way.

Tom: Oh, no. No, if anything, it's been the reverse. We've used materials that are over the top, so they can be described with superlatives in advertising.

Louisa: Hm. Ideally, we should be using stuff that's good for watches and good for marketing as well.

Tom: Sure. But that's easier said than done. I mean, a lot of the materials that are ideal for the job, in terms of scratch-resistance, shock-resistance and all the rest of it, are either pretty ordinary, or their compositions are relatively complex, and they've got complicated names which means they're not all that good for marketing. That's the problem.

Louisa: Sure. But the other problem is, consumers are not technical experts, and they make choices based on their impressions, rather than based on facts. That's a hard commercial fact, as hard as submarine steel.

Tom: No, I accept that.

Louisa: So what should our approach be? It's obviously not an easy question …

2.6

1 not particularly suitable
2 exceptionally resistant
3 not at all suitable
4 tremendously marketable
5 relatively complex
6 not all that good

3.1

Jan: When you look at the various types of plugs and sockets in different countries, most designs have a basic layout that's existed for decades, in terms of the way the pins are laid out, and the profile of the pins. And as a manufacturer, the position of our company has always been, basically, to accept that we're stuck with several standard configurations, and to effectively say to customers, we produce all the main formats – take whichever one you want. However, as I'm sure you know, many countries use plugs and sockets of more than one format. And this leads to a comparative situation, with some configurations becoming more popular, and others progressively being abandoned. This is particularly true in countries undergoing rapid economic expansion. And because of this process of selection, we're finding that big customers are increasingly asking us which of the standard plug and socket formats in current use we recommend as a manufacturer. Which are the best from a technical standpoint? Up until now, we haven't had a standardised company policy to allow us to respond to that question properly. But this project aims to formulate a company policy that allows us to say these are the configurations we recommend, and these are the technical reasons why we recommend them.

3.2

1

Erin: On this one, there are circular pins for live and neutral. There's no earth pin. This is quite a common format in Europe and Russia. It's also quite widely used in India.

2

Erin: Here, you've got circular slots for live and neutral. And the earth slot's got a flat base with one side rounded over to form a semi-circle. This type's only used in a few places.

3

Erin: This one has rectangular blades for live, neutral and earth, in triangular configuration. This is the standard in the UK and Ireland, and a few other places, Malaysia and Singapore, for instance.

4

Erin: This plug has got circular pins for live and neutral, and it has a cylindrical slot to receive the earth pin. It's quite common in continental Europe, and in parts of Africa.

5

Erin: As you can see, there are circular pins for live, neutral and earth, and the pins are arranged in linear configuration. This is not a very commonly used format.

6

Erin: This is the standard in North America, and quite common in Central and South America. Used in Japan, as well. There are flat blades for live and neutral, and a round pin for earth, and they're laid out in triangular configuration. So, an extremely widely used format.

■■■ 3.3

rectangle
rectangular
triangle
triangular
cylinder
cylindrical
line
linear

■■■ 3.4

Erin: In this configuration, there's a circular slot at the top. It's obviously a blind hole, it doesn't go right through. And that's designed to receive the earth pin, which is mounted on the face of the socket. Then there are two plastic ridges, one on either side of the plug casing, and they slot into corresponding grooves at each side of the socket. In addition, the centre of the socket is recessed. So rather than being flush with the front of the socket, on the same face, the circular area that receives the plug is set back from the surrounding casing, in a recess about 15mm deep. The live and neutral sockets are also equipped with covers, just inside the opening. These covers only open when pressure is applied to both by the two pins of the plug simultaneously. So we need to look at the advantages of this configuration …

■■■ 3.5

Andy: In this format the plug slots into the recess in the socket. That allows it to fit in really tightly, compared with other designs. Plus, these ridges and grooves on the sides increase the amount of friction. That helps it to resist pullout forces even more, so it won't fall out of the socket.

Karin: Yeah, but at the end of the day, how securely do you want it to be retained? If it's held in too hard, that makes it difficult to pull out.

Andy: That's true.

Karin: Plus, it could be dangerous. If you're vacuuming enthusiastically to loud music, let's say, and you pull the cord, you actually *want* the plug to pull out, don't you? Otherwise you might rip the cable half way out of the plug, or the appliance.

Andy: So, really, we need to compare the pullout resistance of all the formats.

Karin: And determine what the ideal resistance is.

Andy: Yeah. OK. Erm, what else can we say about this one?

Karin: Well I guess another advantage is, given that the plug's in a recess, if it gets pulled out just a fraction, and the pins are still live, nothing can physically touch them.

Andy: So you think that's more effective than having insulators round the tops of the pins?

Karin: I'd say so, yeah.

Andy: This one's also got covers inside the live and neutral slots.

Karin: That's a standard feature on more or less every format, though, isn't it?

Andy: Yeah. But I think it's something we should look at. I mean, it's obviously a good thing. Anything that stops children from sticking things in is obviously a good idea. The only problem with this system is, if the mechanism's too sensitive, it makes it difficult to insert the plug, sometimes. And that makes it easy to damage.

Karin: When people try to force it.

Andy: Exactly …

■■■ 3.6

Evan: Most of what we do is sheet metal working. We don't do foundry work — you know, casting and that type of thing. That's obviously a different discipline. But apart from that, we're equipped to do most things to do with metal bashing.

Mr Barrett: That's the technical term for it, is it?

Evan: I'm not sure what the technical definition of metal bashing would be. A collective term for hammering, grinding and generally making a lot of noise, probably.

Mr Barrett: It's actually not that noisy in here, is it?

Evan: No, it's not too bad. We had a specialist firm come in a while ago to measure noise levels at each machine — you know, for health and safety regulations. A lot of what we do isn't all that noisy. Things like drilling and milling machines are not too bad, relatively speaking. Anything involving abrasives tends to be noisy, things like grinders, even if they're only hand tools. And that big press over there makes a loud bang when they're shearing steel. It certainly saves a lot of time, though, compared with flame cutting, or sawing with a grinder blade.

Mr Barrett: So, it's a guillotine?

Evan: That's what we use it for mostly, yes.

■■■ 3.7

1

Evan: So we use high-pressure waterjet cutting quite a lot. The good thing about it is you don't need to do any finishing afterwards. The edges are virtually perfect. So they are especially good when you have intricate shapes.

Mr Barrett: Which would be difficult to finish otherwise.

Evan: That's right.

2

Mr Barrett: Saw blades are obviously useless when you're cutting curved shapes.

Evan: That's right. And when you're using any sort of abrasive technique for cutting metal, it inevitably gets hot. And that can alter the properties of the metal around the cut, which can be a problem in some situations.

3

Evan: The other problem with abrasive cutting is it exerts shear forces near the cut. So sawing is not the best solution if you want to avoid altering the material.

Mr Barrett: The same applies to guillotining, presumably.

Evan: It does, yes.

4

Mr Barrett: It's amazing to think that a waterjet can cut through steel. You could imagine water-cutting timber or relatively soft material, but …

Evan: No, it's ideal for metals. Actually, it's not just water that's used. They sometimes add an abrasive powder to the water to increase the cutting power.

Mr Barrett: Oh. I didn't know that.

Evan: The water's obviously concentrated into a very fine jet. Depending on how it's set up, it can take out less than a tenth of a millimetre, sometimes.

Mr Barrett: Really?

■■■ 3.8

Pedro: So, basically, our objective is to get key suppliers more actively involved in the design process. So rather than us going to a supplier and saying, we want a specific type of bolt or screw or rivet for connecting these components, can you give us a price? We want to be able to say, we need a way of joining this part to this part, what's the best way of fixing them to each other?

Alicia: OK.

Pedro: So it might be that you say, well, actually, instead of bolting this onto the machine, what about using a weld? Or instead of riveting these, how about bonding them with adhesive, or fixing them on with some kind of clip, or whatever, whatever's the most cost-effective solution.

Alicia: Right. But, obviously, we're a supplier of mechanical fixings, so we can only provide a mechanical solution. So if you ask us to design some joints, which is obviously quite an involved job, and then, after all that, a rival firm comes along and says, well we suggest welding it all together, or gluing it together for half the price, um, it would mean a lot of work for no return. I'm not saying it's a bad idea. It's just that we would have to be careful we covered our costs.

Pedro: I appreciate that. But the flip side is, we want to work with fewer suppliers than we have in the past. So, overall, that problem would be offset by the greater volume of work you'd get.

Alicia: Hmm.

■■■ 3.9

Lenny: So a typical cluster consists of somewhere in the region of a hundred balloons. That's using ordinary-size weather balloons. With about twenty people helping it takes an hour or so to inflate them all.

Eva: An hour or more with twenty people?

Lenny: Yeah. It's pretty time-consuming.

Eva: And is each balloon tied on individually?

Lenny: That's the way it's often done, yeah.

Eva: And is the rope just fastened around the bottom, or … ?

Lenny: Well, some people use plastic cable ties. Or you can use tape.

Eva: So it's a big job, then, putting everything together. The harness is suspended from a hundred or so ropes, then. Well, how is it fastened?

Lenny: Well, you can put nylon straps beneath the ropes. So you have several ropes tied to a single strap, then each strap is fastened to the harness.

Eva: I see. So it's like a kind of tree structure.

Lenny: That's right. And you have different lengths, so the balloons aren't all at the same level, so they fit above and below one another in a round-shaped cluster.

Eva: I see. So you inflate the balloons, keep tying them to the harness, via the straps, and keep doing that until you take off.

Lenny: Basically, yeah. The pilot's roped to sandbags on the ground. So the balloons are added progressively until there's a marginal amount of lift. Then the anchor ropes are released, and up you go, nice and gently.

Eva: And how do you control your altitude? You carry ballast, presumably.

Lenny: Yes. Water, usually. Those big water bags with taps on, ideally, so it's easy to drain out.

Eva: And how do you come back down to earth?

Lenny: Well, that's actually a reason for having the balloons tied on individually. You can release them, one by one, which allows you to reduce the amount of lift incrementally.

Eva: I see. Because I was thinking, surely it would be easier to just have all the balloons contained within a big net, to make it faster to assemble. You know, rather than spending ages tying every single balloon on individually. But then if you did that, you wouldn't be able to release them, would you?

Lenny: No. That's true.

Eva: You could burst them, somehow, I suppose.

Lenny: Yeah. I mean, there are obviously various ways of doing it …

▰▰ 4.1

Joe: I have a question about the panels on Staircase 3. You know those glass panels around the opening, through Deck C?

Linda: Um, yes. I know where you mean, yeah.

Joe: Well, I've been looking for a cross-section through the deck, at the stair opening. But I can't find one anywhere.

Linda: Isn't there a note on the general arrangement drawing, with a reference to a section on another drawing?

Joe: I couldn't find one.

Linda: I've got the deck plans out, somewhere on here. What's this? Air conditioning schematic, that's no good. Ah here we are. Deck plan. Um, no, you're right. There's no section mentioned.

Joe: I mean, in actual fact, what I need is an elevation, showing all the panels from the front. I thought that might be referenced on the main section through the stairs.

Linda: There is a full set of drawings for all the internal panelling, with details showing exploded views of all the fixing details, and sections through the panel joints. Do you have those?

Joe: Not as far as I know.

Linda: And there's a written specification for the panels, as part of the main spec. That might specify the sizes.

Joe: Those are obviously what I need, then. I want to see how many there are, and what size they are. Have those drawings been issued?

▰▰ 4.2

Pavel: So how wide is this panel at the top?

Joe: Good question. There's no dimension.

Pavel: Is this drawing to scale? It's one to five. Have you got a scale rule? Let's measure it. It looks to be about three hundred mil.

Joe: The golden rule is, you shouldn't scale off drawings, though, should you?

Pavel: Well …

Joe: It's not so bad if it's actual size, on a full-scale drawing, but I'd rather not with this. Let's query it. I'll give them another call in the office.

▰▰ 4.3

Mei: Basically, the client has said they want a superflat finish over the entire floor area. That makes it a free movement floor, where vehicles can run anywhere on it. But on the manufacturing process drawings, it shows precisely specified routes for these automated vehicles. So, technically, it should be a defined movement floor, where you can just have a few narrow lanes for the vehicles, which are superflat, and then the rest of the slab is just laid to normal tolerances.

Lewis: Right. So you're questioning the extra cost of doing everything superflat?

Mei: That's the main thing, yeah. The other thing is quality. To get the best finish on these superflat floors, it's better to lay narrow widths of slab in fairly long lengths. So, ideally, you want lanes, rather than big, wide areas.

Lewis: OK. But maybe they want everywhere to be superflat so they can change the layout of the production line in the future.

Mei: Possibly. But even if they want to do that, the surface can always be modified at a later date. It's a thick slab, so there's nothing to stop them grinding a layer off the top. In fact, we could increase the depth of the steel reinforcement slightly when we pour the slab, so there's some extra thickness of concrete over it. So, if they did want to grind a thin layer off a section in future, they wouldn't have problems with shallow cover.

Lewis: Right. Well let's look into an alternative design for a defined movement floor.

▰▰ 4.4

1
Leo: I've worked on projects in the past where every single working drawing is circulated to every team – structural, mechanical and electrical – and it just gets completely out of control. So we want to avoid that situation.

Engineer 1: Sure. But after saying that, if someone has to analyse every single revision to determine exactly which team needs it, then that takes a lot of time as well.

Leo: Not if there's a proper procedure in place. As long as we make sure there's …

2
Leo: This project strikes one as pretty complex, in terms of the amount of integration and overlap between the different design packages.

Engineer 1: Yeah.

Leo: Particularly between mechanical and electrical teams so we have to coordinate that. And it's obviously a specialist job. It's beyond my expertise as the overall project manager. So, in order to make sure that we …

3
Leo: Thinking about how the separate design groups work together, I don't want to rely too much on scheduled meetings. We don't want questions and problems piling up, waiting to be resolved at a meeting in a week's time, or whenever. You all need to be talking to one another on an ongoing basis.

Engineer 2: I agree with what you're saying. The trouble is, when you're trying to sort out problems with details on drawings and that kind of thing, you need to meet face-to-face. And given that we all work in separate offices, it's, you know, we can phone each other, but …

Engineer 1: Yeah, you still need meetings.

Engineer 2: Especially as there's so much integration between the different packages, the point we were talking about before.

Leo: Well, there is a solution to the problem.

▰▰ 4.5

Leo: So, to sum up. As regards design information flow, all preliminary drawings are going to be shown to the senior engineer in charge of each design team. The senior engineers then say whether or not their teams need to receive copies of later revisions. If they don't, they won't receive any further revisions. If they do, they'll be issued with every subsequent revision and, later, revisions of working drawings. To coordinate the interface between mechanical and electrical design, I'm going to appoint a mechanical and electrical coordinator responsible for liaising between the senior engineers in the teams, reporting to me. We're locating all three design teams in a single, open-plan office so when anyone's got a question or a problem, they can talk to the appropriate person face-to-face. We still have scheduled meetings to discuss formal issues, but the emphasis will be on ongoing, informal dialogue between the teams.

▰▰ 4.6

Chen: There's a discrepancy between these details that you might be able to clarify straight away. On the plan of this plate, it shows eight bolts. But on section A, here, there are no bolts shown in the middle. So there would only be six, which obviously contradicts the plan. But as you can see, this plate's going to be bolted to a T profile. So we couldn't put a row of bolts down the middle, because they'd clash with the flange running along the middle of the T. So I'd propose just going for two rows of bolts. The alternative would be to redesign the T section, which obviously would be a bigger job.

Ron: Yes. Let's go for two rows of bolts, as per the sections.

Chen: OK, fine. Will you send an email to confirm that?

▰▰ 5.1

Sabino: A race is not just a test of speed, but the ultimate test of reliability. There's an old saying, *to finish first, first you must finish*, and it's especially true in endurance racing. You're not just competing against rival teams, you're also fighting what you could call engineering enemies, which can cause parts of the car to fail, things like heat, pressure, vibration, shocks, abrasion – there's continual stress on almost all the components, all the nuts and bolts on the car. The chassis, engine, gearbox and clutch, suspension, brakes, tyres, wings, cooling system – they all have to cope with phenomenal levels of wear and tear.

▰▰ 5.2

Sabino: Just to give you some examples of the types of technical problems we've had so far at this test. On one of the cars, a nut worked loose on a radiator pipe, which resulted in coolant liquid leaking out. That caused the engine to start overheating. Fortunately, the driver saw the warning light come on, and he switched off before the system had run out of coolant. Then on the other car we had a fuel feed problem; the engine cut out on one of the corners. That caused the driver to spin off. We were fortunate, he didn't hit anything. But when the car goes off the circuit, the openings in the side pods always clog up with dirt. So those had to be cleaned out. Obviously, you don't want anything blocking the airflow to the radiators. And then because of the spin, the rubber was flat spotted. The tyres weren't close to wearing out, but they still had to be changed, because of the flat spots. And then while they were putting the wheels back on after that, they had a wheel nut jam, it wouldn't turn. And that's actually how problems tend to happen, very often. You get a kind of chain of events, when you feel that everything's going against you. Having said that, you could also say we were lucky. Fortunately, the radiator problem didn't cause the engine to blow up. And after the spin, luckily he didn't hit the barriers and bend the suspension or snap it completely. And even more fortunately, it didn't crack the tub – the chassis.

5.3

Al: So what does the warning message say?

Mr Rooney: When you start the engine, it says check injection.

Al: Right.

Mr Rooney: Obviously, it must be some sort of defect in the fuel injection system. The thing is, though, it only happens intermittently. Sometimes, you start it and there's no message at all. So it might be a software problem, I don't know. Or maybe it could be a defective sensor.

Al: Is the engine working properly?

Mr Rooney: It seems to be fine, yeah.

Al: It doesn't appear to be misfiring or down on power?

Mr Rooney: No, we haven't noticed anything. Presumably, it can't be anything too serious. We thought it was possibly water in the fuel system because it's an outdoor unit. But in that case, I assume there'd be major problems with it.

Al: Has it been refuelled recently?

Mr Rooney: Not that recently.

Al: And was it refuelled with diesel stored in your own tank, or directly from a delivery tanker?

Mr Rooney: From a tanker truck.

Al: I doubt it's water, then, if the fuel went in directly from a delivery. You said the warning doesn't display systematically?

Mr Rooney: No.

Al: In what sort of circumstances does it come up?

Mr Rooney: Well, when you start it up for the first time each day, it comes up. But then if you stop it, and start it again a short time after, there's no message. It's when it's been off for a long time that you get the message.

Al: OK. So it's certainly a question of temperature. It only comes up when it's started from cold?

Mr Rooney: Um, yeah. Exactly.

Al: Hm, it sounds like it's a faulty fuel pre-heater. It's probably just one of the pre-heater plugs that's gone. It's only a minor fault.

Mr Rooney: Oh, right. So it doesn't need urgent attention?

Al: No. It can be replaced at the next service. Keep an eye on it, though. If any other problems start to show up give us a call and we'll send someone over.

5.4

Alan: Hello.

Julia: Hello Alan, it's Julia. I've just started a landing gear check and found a bit of a problem with some tyres. All the pressures on one of the wing blocks are well down.

Alan: On the same block?

Julia: Yeah. On all the other blocks they're correct. So it seems odd that this one group of tyres, on one corner of the aircraft, are all low. And the strange thing is, they're down by exactly the same amount on every tyre on the block.

Alan: I see. You're right, that is unusual.

Julia: The wear rate's consistent across the whole aircraft, though. There's nothing unusual about the wear pattern.

Alan: Are you sure the pressure gauge is working properly?

Julia: Um, well, to be honest you can tell just by looking at the tyres that they're down.

Alan: Right. Let me come out and have a look.

5.5

Paul: OK, let's have a look at the coolant, first. The level's OK.

Eric: It's full of residue, though, by the look of it.

Paul: It looks a bit black, doesn't it? Time to change it, I think.

Eric: OK. What's the filter like?

Paul: Um … it looks reasonable to me.

Eric: Is it due to be changed?

Paul: It is if we follow the service programme to the letter. The trouble is, if you do that, you end up wasting parts half of the time.

Eric: We can take it out and give it a bit of a clean. It'll be alright.

Paul: OK. Blades, next. Hm, they look more or less OK to me. There are no signs of damage.

Eric: Yeah. No need to change those. They'll have moved a bit since they were last checked, though. The alignment will need to be looked at.

Paul: Sure.

Eric: Apart from that, it's not looking too bad.

6.1

Claudia: So with regard to the capacity, in terms of the number of people it actually needs to carry, what sort of figure are you looking at?

Kevin: Um, 36 is what we're aiming for.

Dave: If you think we can add a few seats without making compromises, then by all means, let's look at it.

Kevin: I think 36 is going to be at the top end as far as size is concerned.

Claudia: And as regards the graphics, is the video sequence finalised? Will it be exactly as it is on this DVD?

Kevin: Unless you have any problems generating the physical effects that go with it, then, yeah, as far as we're concerned, that's it.

Claudia: Right, excellent. We can start looking at that straight away then, and get things moving. Um, so regarding the schedule, then, what sort of timescale do you have in mind, for the whole project?

6.2

Claudia: In terms of the physical effects, to what extent do you want the experience to be physical? The degree to which it moves can be varied quite considerably.

Kevin: Well, I mean, we want it to be physical, that's why we're having a dynamic simulator. But we obviously don't want it to be so extreme that people are closing their eyes and not watching the amazing graphics we've got.

Claudia: Sure. I mean, it's obviously difficult to quantify something like this, in theory, sitting in a meeting room. The only way to determine what's right is to actually sit in a simulator and experience it yourself, in practice.

Dave: Of course.

Claudia: So what I'd suggest is, after the meeting we can strap you into one of our machines, and you can assess the possibilities.

Kevin: Sounds interesting!

6.3

Rick: It obviously has to be lifted with a crane.

Gabriella: Yes, but do the slings necessarily have to pass under the base? Why not come up with a way of hooking onto the side of the statue?

Rick: How?

Gabriella: Well, couldn't we drill into it, horizontally, and insert bars into the holes? Then hook onto the bars.

Rick: People would see the holes afterwards, though.

Gabriella: We could fill all the holes, couldn't we? Surely they could use some sort of filler that's the same colour as the stone.

Rick: They'd never hide the holes completely, though. It would still leave marks, wouldn't it? I don't think that would be acceptable.

Gabriella: Or, alternatively, we could make sure the holes were out of sight. What about drilling into the top, vertically? If the holes were right on the top, they'd be less visible. Then the bars could be set in, with lifting eyes on the end.

Rick: Hmm. The trouble is, if the bars were set in with resin, they'd never come out. They'd have to be cut off, wouldn't they? And this mammoth's lying down, so the top will probably be seen, to an extent.

Gabriella: True.

Rick: To be honest, I don't think we can envisage drilling into it. I suppose another option would be to use some sort of grab, on the end of the crane jib. You know, like the ones they use for offloading lorries. So, the statue would be held by friction. But I can't imagine there being anything capable of lifting 36 tonnes. Especially not something that wide.

Gabriella: Hm, no. Have you spoken to the masons about this?

Rick: Not yet, no.

Gabriella: Why don't we ask them?

6.4

Viktor: So all the steel beams shown on this drawing are going to be fixed to the walls, bolted through the concrete.

Rajesh: Right.

Viktor: So to bolt through, obviously we need holes in the walls. We can core drill them, with a diamond drill, which would obviously be done after the walls have been cast. Um, we'd drill them ourselves, as part of our contract package. Alternatively, the holes can be preformed by putting plastic tubes into the concrete when they cast the walls, in which case the contractor responsible for the concrete structure would do the job.

Rajesh: OK.

Viktor: Now, the problem is, these bolts won't have much play.

Rajesh: How do you mean?

Viktor: Well, they've got to fit quite tightly in the holes, so they won't be able to move much. There won't be much space around them, to adjust their position.

Rajesh: I see.

Viktor: So that means the holes have got to be positioned very precisely. If they're slightly out of position on the wall, they won't match up with the holes that have been pre-drilled through the steel beams, at our factory.

Rajesh: Sure.

Viktor: That's the main technical issue, in terms of deciding how we form these holes. Obviously, the technical side's not the only consideration. There's also the question of timescales – given that there are a lot of these holes to do. And, obviously, the question of cost, as well.

■ 6.5

Viktor: In terms of cost, preforming is obviously a lot cheaper, because all you need are plastic tubes, which are cheap to buy, and quick to put in. If we do it that way, it'll be dead easy, and it'll cost peanuts. Whereas core drilling will be slow, it'll be quite a painstaking job. But …

Rajesh: But core drilling's more accurate, clearly.

Viktor: A lot more accurate. I mean, sometimes, you can get away with preforming. If you need to get within twenty mil, then it's perfectly feasible. Ten mil is – it's achievable, but it's stretching it. Anything less than ten mil, and there's no way you can do it.

Rajesh: And what sort of tolerance are you looking for?

Viktor: About ten mil.

Rajesh: So it's borderline, then.

Viktor: It's a tall order. The safe bet would be going for core drilling.

Rajesh: The problem is going to be the schedule, though.

Viktor: Exactly. I mean, to diamond drill the number of holes we're talking about will take, um …

Rajesh: It'll take forever and a day, won't it? Whereas if they're preformed, they'd be ready as soon as the walls are cast.

Viktor: But if half of them are in the wrong place, it'll cost an arm and a leg to put them right. Because if they're wrong, it's not just a question of drilling new ones in the right place. If they're slightly out of position, they have to be filled in, first, with cement, to avoid having two holes overlapping. So putting them right is easier said than done.

Rajesh: Sure. So as I see it, the key issue here, in terms of feasibility, is the tolerance. If the holes can be bigger, and there's more play for the bolts, we won't have this problem.

■ 6.6

Marta: So, to be clear about how far we can go with this redesign, we're not aiming to reinvent the wheel, in terms of the main components and how they fit together. The reasons for that are firstly, from a hardware point of view, the existing design has proved to be effective. And secondly, we don't have the resources at this point in time to make fundamental changes to the production process.

Engineer 1: So the overall internal layout needs to remain the same?

Marta: Yes. We're looking for an evolution, rather than designing the whole thing from the ground up. Presumably, there is room for improvement?

Engineer 2: Well, this model has been revamped once before, of course. But, no doubt we can refine it a bit more.

Marta: However, given that software redesign isn't an assembly issue and has been the Achilles heel of the existing model, it would make sense to rethink that whole system.

Engineer 1: So for software, back to the drawing board, then?

Marta: Well, er, whatever we do, we need to make a quantum leap. Whether that means designing the system from scratch, I don't know. We need to make the whole thing much simpler to use.

■ 7.1

a

Rosana: Next week they're due to start maintenance work on the grain silos in Zone 4. We need to make sure that everyone's aware that all those silos are classed as confined spaces. In other words, no one should go inside them without first doing an air test. And we need to keep a check on dust levels, as well.

Marc: We've got a CO_2 detector here, haven't we?

b

Rosana: If you walk past that machine while it's running, and you're trying to talk to someone, you have to shout to be heard. And as a rule of thumb, that means it should be an ear protection area.

Marc: Yeah, but the regs differentiate between brief exposure, when you're walking past something, and continuous exposure, don't they?

c

Marc: So is it harmful if it splashes on your skin?

Rosana: According to the notice it's an irritant, and it's toxic.

Marc: But it's not corrosive?

Rosana: Not as far as I'm aware.

Marc: So you don't need gloves and eye protection and masks and all the rest of it? If you get any on your skin, you just wash it off.

Rosana: Hm, I'm not sure about that.

d

Rosana: We need to enquire whether or not this maintenance involves welding. There are forklift trucks going through that area carrying flammable liquids. If there are going to be any naked flames or sparks, we'll need to put a proper procedure in place.

Marc: Right. I'll get in touch with their people, then.

■ 7.2

Stephanie: So in terms of access, theoretically, there's a risk of someone falling, as they climb up a silo, or down into one. But there's always an external staircase with a guardrail, leading to the top, and there are permanent ladders, with protective hoops around them, fixed to the insides, leading down to the bottom. So workers should be able to access these silos fairly safely. The big problem will be getting the welding equipment, the gas bottles, down into the bottom.

Ben: They can be lowered down by rope.

Stephanie: Won't they be too heavy?

Ben: Not if they use the smaller-sized bottles.

Stephanie: We'll need to specify the bottle size in the procedure, then.

Ben: Yeah. They'll have to take care that the bottles don't fall onto someone, as well. That no one's standing in the bottom of the silo, while they lower them down.

Stephanie: True. That's another point to mention. OK, so access isn't really a problem, then. The main danger is the fact that it's a confined space. Especially given that they're welding, with an oxy acetylene torch burning, which will produce a fair amount of CO_2.

Ben: So they'll need a CO_2 detector.

Stephanie: I mean, to be safe, they'll need to test the air before they go down, anyway. But we should probably specify that they need to keep the detector with them while they're working, and keep it switched on.

Ben: Yeah. Another hazard is there'll be metal fumes given off as they're actually welding, which is a different problem to the CO_2 issue.

Stephanie: Sure. So really, they'll need a ventilation system down there, some kind of air extractor.

Ben: Probably, yeah. And there's the problem of dust, as well. They'll have to be very careful about that. If they're welding and there's grain dust in the air, there's going to be an explosion hazard.

Stephanie: Yeah. Would a ventilator clear the dust, or make it worse? I suppose if there's a lot lying around, it'd keep blowing it up into the air, wouldn't it?

Ben: Mm. I'm not sure.

■ 7.3

Stephanie: Restricted areas are places where a serious danger is present. So it's essential that these should be kept locked at all times. Under no circumstances should anyone be able to access them, unless they have a permit to work, in other words, a written form giving permission to work in the restricted area.

Lin: And permits to work, and the keys to restricted areas, can only be issued by the electrical supervisor?

Stephanie: That's right. So that one individual is responsible for electrical safety for the whole plant. Only that person is authorised to issue permits to work.

Lin: Presumably, it's important that permits are issued every single time someone enters a restricted area – each time they do a new job, they need a new permit.

Stephanie: Exactly. They shouldn't be issued for any longer than a full shift.

Lin: OK.

Stephanie: And it's crucial that there's just a single key to each restricted area. The whole idea of having a lock-out system is to ensure that only one person has access to switchgear at any given time. So whatever happens, someone cannot switch on a circuit at a switchboard while somebody else is working on it somewhere else in the plant.

Lin: Mm, if we imagine a technician needs to, let's say they're going to change a motor on one of the lines, they get a permit to work, and obtain the key to the switchboard from the electrical supervisor. Then they take the key, unlock the door to the switchboard, switch off the circuit-breaker for the motor, to isolate it, then lock the door again.

Stephanie: That's right. Then, while they're working, it's vital that they keep the key on them continuously.

7.4

Krisztof: The main hazard, when manoeuvring a helicopter close to power lines, is the risk of a collision with the line. So before commencing work, it's essential for the crew to have detailed information about weather conditions, especially wind direction and speed. Operating in very windy weather is obviously out of the question. The pilots involved in live line work are highly trained and experienced and their expertise is arguably the crucial factor in ensuring safety. Another hazard is snagging, as at certain times the platform will momentarily be attached to the power line and to the helicopter, leaving the aircraft tethered. It's essential, therefore, that the cable is equipped with a tension release mechanism, so that if the helicopter pulls away suddenly for any reason, the cable can break free. To prevent electrocution and burns from arcing currents, the crew on the platform wear hot suits. These have stainless-steel threads which channel the electricity around the technician's body, allowing the 400,000 volt supply to flow between the power line and the platform. The suits also have a fireproof lining, to provide protection from heat. And eye protection is worn, as a protection against flashes from electric arcs. Again, training is one of the key factors in ensuring safety. As a precaution against mechanical failure, the suspension cable, platform and all associated equipment are systematically inspected before each operation, to check for damage. And the helicopter is maintained in line with aviation regulations. One additional precaution is taken regarding the helicopter's engines: only twin-engine craft are used for live line work, so that if an engine fails, the pilot can still land safely.

7.5

Isobel: The focus of the course will be on your personal obligations in terms of looking after your own safety, and the safety of others. That means we'll be focusing on specific safety regulations. For instance, we'll be looking at personal protective equipment that's compulsory Or activities that are prohibited in certain areas, such as smoking. The majority of the obligations we'll deal with are legal requirements. In other words, they're stipulated by law as part of health and safety legislation. If you contravene these kinds of regulations, it's not the same as turning up for work late, or merely breaching your contract of employment in some way. If someone fails to comply with health and safety regs, they're breaking the law. It's as simple as that. I'm sure you're all aware of that, but it is an important point to emphasise.

7.6

1

Petrus: If there's a fire, you shouldn't use water extinguishers on this machine, because it contains electrical circuits, and it can cause electrocution. You should only use a carbon dioxide extinguisher.

2

Petrus: When you lift this machine, it's essential that you should only use the two lifting eyes marked in red. No other parts of the frame are load-bearing, so you mustn't use them as anchor points.

3

Petrus: You should take care when you're cleaning below the guillotine blade, because there's a danger that the blade could come down. Before you clean it, you should always set the control lever in the Blade Locked position. And you should wear protective gloves while you're cleaning it, because the sump below the blade can contain sharp metal off-cuts.

8.1

Roland: We know the client is a very green orientated company, very big on all things environmental.

Saskia: Absolutely.

Roland: So energy saving obviously needs to be an important consideration in the design. Clearly, it's a big subject, and something we need to look into in depth. But one specific aspect of it where I think we can make a real difference is with the Building Management System – specifically, with the way we use presence detectors. And I've had a couple of ideas that I'd appreciate your views on.

Saskia: Sure.

Roland: I think we should put two totally different design options to the client. Option one is to have a building with maximum automation. So with the maximum automation option …

8.2

Roland: … with the maximum automation option, we put presence detectors all over the place, and link them to as many systems as possible. Not just the usual systems that activate the lights when people walk into rooms and turn them off when they leave. We could use presence detectors to control other systems, as well, like the blinds on the windows. So, if it's the middle of summer, and a presence detector senses that everyone's left a meeting room, a temperature sensor picks up a positive reading from sunlight coming through the glass, the electronics activate the blinds, which automatically come down and black out the room. That would limit heat absorption and reduce the load on the air-conditioning, saving energy.

Saskia: OK.

Roland: Or in winter, if the blinds had been pulled down in the meeting room the evening before, the next morning, the sensor detects sunlight, and triggers the blinds to raise and let in as much sunlight as possible, contributing to the heating. And there could be temperature measurements to determine which rooms are the warmest, and those sensors set off a circulation system to distribute the warm air through the building, into the corridor, or into rooms at the other side of the building, or wherever.

Saskia: So, we'd use presence detectors and heat sensors to regulate as many systems as possible?

Roland: Yes. Well, that's what we'd have with the maximum automation option.

8.3

Roland: The second option is this. It's a very environmentally conscious company, so I assume that green attitude is shared by all the staff. If that's the case, why is there a need to automate everything in the building when most things can be operated manually? Why doesn't the boss just circulate an email reminding people to switch the lights off when they go out and tell them to lower the blinds when they leave a room in summer, so it helps the air-conditioning? I mean, you'd save

electricity, because you wouldn't need to control all the systems automatically, and the money you saved by buying old-fashioned manual controls instead of hi-tech electronics could be spent on planting trees or something. I mean, it sounds simple, but …

Saskia: Mm … it's a very interesting idea. We have to bear in mind, of course, that the client's a manufacturer of hi-tech electronic gizmos. I'm not sure how they'd feel about …

8.4

1

Jochem: The obvious danger here is that you could get a build-up inside the vessel if there's a blockage further along the pipe.

Katerina: So the vessel needs a safety valve?

Jochem: Yes, and maybe some sort of warning system, as well. It could be something that's triggered by a differential measurement. So if there's a high reading in the tank, and a lower one further along, you'd know there was a blockage somewhere.

2

Katerina: We'll need a system for monitoring gas consumption.

Jochem: What, a meter on the supply pipe?

Katerina: Well, yes, that would measure cumulative consumption. But we also need to monitor the actual rate of consumption at different points in time during the reaction cycle. And if we have those two parameters, we can then determine the frequency of peaks in consumption, which is the third parameter we need.

Jochem: So that's a software issue, then. As long as the cumulative value's being recorded against the timescale, we can plot the rate of consumption …

3

Katerina: The reaction that takes place is going to be exothermic. But the amount of heat will partly depend on how hot the gas is when it enters the vessel.

Jochem: Yes, because that input heat can be adjusted.

Katerina: Exactly. So we'll need a sensor next to the valve to measure the input value, as gas comes in, and then another to give us an output value. Then, we can work out the optimum input temperature for the gas.

8.5

Helen: One of the biggest headaches in power generation is the fact that electricity consumption fluctuates considerably. So in order to maintain a continuous supply we have to make continual checks, and adjust the power load we generate. To help us plan those adjustments, we forecast fluctuations in demand, so that we can anticipate peaks and troughs. We base these forecasts on a number of different factors. One of them, one of the most important ones, is temperature. During periods of very cold or very hot weather, demand increases. The increase in demand is obviously due to millions of electric radiators coming on when it's cold, and air-conditioning units working hard when it's hot. Another factor, a key factor which increases or decreases demand, is whether or not it's light or dark in the morning and evening – obviously that dictates lighting consumption. So those are the two main seasonal factors. They generally go hand-in-hand so on cold, dark, winter evenings, the rise in demand is significant, compared with warm, light, summer evenings. We also take into account what day of the week it is, particularly whether it's a weekday or the weekend. Generally, demand rises during the week, when factories and offices are operational, and then decreases when a lot of them close at the end of the week. So demand falls at the weekend. Those are variations that take place within a given week. During any given day, there are factors such as mealtimes, when electric ovens are switched on – obviously, that causes a jump in consumption. Even commercial breaks during popular TV shows can cause blips in demand. There can be a sudden rise when people rush to switch kettles on, or heat up snacks in microwaves, and then a sudden fall shortly afterwards.

8.6

Helen: Because electricity consumption fluctuates across a significant range, in order to cope with peak demand our maximum capacity is equivalent to the top of that band of fluctuation. That means that during off-peak periods, we have significant spare generating capacity. Now, in an ideal world, it would be good to use that spare capacity to generate power and store it for use during peak times. Unfortunately, as you probably know, electrical charge is extremely difficult to store in large amounts – you can't just charge up huge batteries. So we use an innovative technique to store up power potential during off-peak periods.

8.7

Helen: The concept of pumped storage is relatively simple. During off-peak periods when main power stations have got spare capacity, some of the extra power they produce is used by pumped storage stations to pump water from a low-level reservoir up to a high-level reservoir, where the water's stored. It's then held there until there's a peak in demand at some point the next day. At that point, the water's released, and it flows down the pipes, driving turbines at the bottom which generate electricity. Obviously, the station can only run for a fairly short period, but it's sufficient to cover the peak in demand. Then, as soon as there's a dip in demand, the water can be pumped back up and held ready for use again. So the effect is to smooth out fluctuations in the output of the main power stations. Some of the main stations' spare capacity is used when there would be a trough in the demand curve, at night. The peak daytime generating capacity of those main stations can also be lower because the pumped storage stations are there to back them up when there are blips in the demand curve.

8.8

Gerry: Questionnaires like this drive me mad. I mean, look at this first question. What percentage of my time do I spend doing technical tasks that use my skills extensively? How are you supposed to put a number against that?

Eleanor: You only need to give a ballpark figure.

Gerry: I know, but even so. It's difficult to say, off the top of my head.

Eleanor: It's easier if you compare it with the second option.

Gerry: Doing tasks that a less qualified colleague could do. Well, let's say roughly half and half.

Eleanor: Are you sure? Aren't you the least qualified person in this department?

Gerry: Do you know, I knew you were going to say that. Number two – technical tasks that add value and tasks that don't add value, such as admin. Add value? What's that supposed to …

Eleanor: Well, do you not do some admin? Or do you spend all of your time doing productive things?

Gerry: Well, no. Nowhere near all of it.

Eleanor: Right. So is it fifty-fifty?

Gerry: Um well, no. I spend more time problem solving than I do on admin. Thankfully. Let's say somewhere in the region of two thirds. So, about a third on admin. Three – tasks that are purely technical versus tasks that relate to technical organisation. Well, most of what I do is organisation, isn't it? I spend pretty much all my time on that.

Eleanor: Or in your case, disorganisation.

Gerry: Nice one. What figure did you put down for added value, by the way? Was it a negative number?

8.9

Beatrice: At this stage, I'm not asking you to give me a detailed breakdown of all the IT equipment we're going to need. It would just be useful to have a rough idea of what's most urgent.

Dan: Sure. Well, one of the biggest problems is the screens at the CAD stations. A lot of those need replacing with bigger ones. Roughly speaking, I'd say well over half of them are too small. A good two thirds of them, actually. So, we're talking about 15 to 18 screens, something like that.

Beatrice: OK. How urgent is that?

Dan: Well, I mean they all work, they all function properly. The trouble is, the engineers spend the vast majority of their time working with these screens. And because the detail on them is so small, it's pretty hard work on the eyes, to the point that it affects productivity so …

Beatrice: OK. And what about the big printer in here? I've heard it's a bit of a dinosaur.

Dan: Well, it is, but it works perfectly well, and we print next to nothing with it, anyway. Most of the drawings are printed at the factory.

Beatrice: Oh.

9.1

Tony: With the aerodynamics there are three development tools available to us. The first is CFD software – Computational Fluid Dynamics. With that, the tests would obviously be virtual, based on a computer model. The second option is to go into a wind tunnel, with a scale model, or a full-size mock-up. In either case, we'd probably need to use a tunnel with a rolling road.

Lisa: Would that be necessary?

Tony: Well, the thing is, the wheels generate a lot of turbulence when they're spinning. So to simulate that, you need a rolling road.

Lisa: Yes, I know, but if we go for a bodywork design where the wheels are mostly enclosed, which is likely, would that be an issue?

Tony: Possibly not. It depends how fully enclosed they are.

Lisa: OK. I'm just raising the question.

Tony: Sure. It's something we can look at. The third option, then, is field testing, actually running the prototype outside on a runway, or somewhere. So we can use these tools in isolation or as a combination. The question is, how can we gather as much data as possible with the limited budget we have?

Guy: Well, we need to bear in mind that the problem with aero is that it's not just about data gathering. You also have to validate the data. CFD and wind tunnels are not a hundred percent reliable. The acid test only comes when you try out a full-scale prototype in real conditions. We need to make sure that everything is tried-and-tested outside, with a full-scale trial run.

Lisa: Yeah, but let's not forget we're designing a car that does a hundred kilometres an hour, it's not a supersonic aircraft! The aero's not going to be that critical.

Tony: Plus, with changeable weather, it's not easy to do back-to-back testing out in the field.

Guy: No, of course not. I'm just saying we need to be careful …

9.2

Arnaud: So, theoretically, the horizontal speed will keep decreasing until the container hits the ground. The higher the drop altitude, the lower the horizontal speed at touchdown.

Jenna: Sure.

Arnaud: But, obviously, the higher the altitude, the higher the vertical speed, up to a certain point.

Jenna: Absolutely. So, assuming the drop altitude's very low, the vertical speed won't be all that high on impact.

Arnaud: True.

Jenna: And in terms of protecting the cargo, surely a low vertical speed is the critical factor.

Arnaud: I'm not so sure it's the critical factor. I'd say the horizontal speed's more problematic. Because, presumably, if the groundspeed's quite high, there's a danger the container will roll over and bounce along when it touches down. In fact, if you're dropping from low altitude, that's probably inevitable. So if the container rolled and bounced for 50 metres, or whatever, then you'd have to have some kind of destructible external envelope to protect it from the multiple impacts. Which would be very expensive. So, arguably, rolling is the worst problem, worse than a high vertical impact speed.

Jenna: Hm, you think so?

Arnaud: So you don't think rolling's a bad thing?

Jenna: I'm not convinced the container would actually roll.

Arnaud: No?

Jenna: Not necessarily. The military drop tanks out of flying aircraft at low level, tied to special platforms, and they just slide along the ground. And the systems that eject things out of the backs of planes are incredibly powerful. So because, obviously, they fire the container in the opposite direction to the plane, that reduces the groundspeed. Plus, they use a parachute that deploys horizontally, which also helps to slow it down.

Arnaud: Of course.

Jenna: So, based on what they do with tanks, I think we can safely assume that we can stop a container from rolling.

Arnaud: But a tank's got massive weight, and a low centre of gravity. With a smaller, lighter container, there's no way of knowing how it would behave, not without actually testing it. And even if you tested it ten times, it would probably behave differently each time, it would be very unpredictable. Whereas if you drop from a higher altitude, OK, the vertical speed is higher, but with a lower groundspeed, it would behave more predictably. And that would make it easier to design a cushioning system because you'd be dealing with a single, predictable impact.

Jenna: Yes, but surely, a heavy vertical landing is a huge problem. The force of it would be far greater …

▬ 9.3

Manfred: The first time we launched one of these things, er, we basically just got a plastic washing-up liquid bottle, filled it about half full of water, then pumped it up with an ordinary foot pump.

Interviewer: So it was just ordinary household stuff?

Manfred: Oh, yeah, nothing too technical. And, actually, there was a bit of a coincidence, because the opening in the bottle was just slightly bigger than the fitting at the end of the pump, so there was quite a good seal. So we pumped it up – one of us held the bottle while someone else worked the pump. And we released it, and it went up, literally, like a rocket. I mean, we expected it would shoot up reasonably fast, but we didn't anticipate just how powerful it would be. It just went *whoosh* and totally exceeded our expectations. So you can imagine us, a group of 12-year-olds, we were absolutely ecstatic. And having said that, there was one problem. Once all the water had come out, which happened virtually in a split-second, the bottle – because it was very light – started tumbling over in the air.

Interviewer: So it wouldn't fly straight?

Manfred: That's right. But we quickly came up with a solution to that problem.

▬ 9.4

Manfred: What we did was to get a plastic cup, a strong one not a disposable cup, and pushed it onto the end of the bottle, at the top, to form a nose. It didn't go exactly according to plan, at first. It stabilised it a bit, but it still wasn't flying straight. So we tried putting water in the beaker, to act as ballast, and that worked a treat. With the extra inertia, and the fact that it was front-heavy, it went like an arrow. So, so, yes, we sorted that problem out. Then the next goal was to increase the power, to try and reach a higher altitude.

▬ 9.5

Manfred: One of the things we did was to experiment with the amount of water inside the bottle. I think, initially, we expected that the more water we put in, the more powerful it would be. But as it turned out, it was the opposite. What actually happened was, if you overfilled it, there wasn't enough pressure to expel all the water. We reduced the amount of water to about a quarter or a third full, something like that, and we also put some tape around the end of the pump, to get a better seal with the bottle. That was really effective. I think we underestimated the pressure we were generating. And, certainly, we were overestimating the strength of the bottle. Because it got to the point where we were firing these rockets up to, I don't know, maybe something like 20 metres high, something like that, so you can imagine the sort of pressure involved. And plastic bottles are hardly up to the job of high-pressure rocketry, obviously. So, inevitably, the bottle eventually blew up while I was holding it. I was rolling around on the ground with sore hands, while everyone else was rolling about laughing. So I learned the hard way.

▬ 9.6

Caroline: So how credible is this hoax theory, then? I watched a documentary about it a while ago.

Renato: Well, some of the questions are quite interesting, but from what I've read, they can all be explained, scientifically. You know, like the fact that the stars aren't visible in the sky on the photos. Apparently, it's just due to sunlight on the surface of the moon. It was too bright to see them, that's all.

Caroline: Isn't the flag supposedly waving in the wind, in one of the shots?

Renato: That's right, yeah. They say it's because of the pole shaking after it'd been stuck in. There's obviously no air, so as a result, it kept moving for ages, due to the fact that there was no friction to slow it down.

Caroline: I see.

Renato: Another thing that's been explained is the footprints on the surface. People had said the ground looked wet, so it couldn't have been on the moon. But, apparently, that's the way that type of dust behaves in a vacuum. It sticks together, like mud.

Caroline: Wasn't there some other theory to do with dust when the module landed, that there should have been more dust, or something?

Renato: Well, during the landing, there was supposedly a lot of dust flying up, you know, caused by the blast from the engines. But when the module's actually seen on the surface, there's no crater visible below it. So the theory is that, if it had really landed there, it would have left a crater. But the argument against that is that it had already slowed down substantially by the time it reached the surface, and it was only descending gently, because of the low gravity.

Caroline: So there was only a bit of surface dust blown up?

Renato: That's right.

▬ 10.1

Mike: Obviously, a tubular steel tower only gives you sufficient structural strength if you give it adequate protection from corrosion – the big problem with offshore installations. So, technically, you could say steel is inappropriate in that environment.

Loreta: They make ships out of it.

Mike: I know, Loreta, but only because there's no cost-effective alternative. But we're not talking about ships, we're talking about fixed structures. The point is, I think we should look more seriously at alternatives to all-steel supports. And the obvious alternative is reinforced concrete.

Loreta: We've already looked into it, though, and it wasn't cost-effective.

Mike: Not in the short term. But we didn't really look into it properly over the long term.

Loreta: But you made the point yourself, Mike, that steel's completely ineffective if it's corroded. And one of the main constituents of reinforced concrete is steel.

Mike: It's protected, though, isn't it? It's embedded inside concrete. That's a much more effective protection than paint.

Loreta: Not necessarily. If we're talking about the long term, as you say, what happens to concrete when it's exposed to the sea for a few years? It erodes. Which means the steel eventually gets exposed. You look at concrete coastal defences. How often do you see the concrete all crumbling away, and all the steel exposed?

Mike: That's due to inconsistent quality, though. You only get that problem if there's insufficient cover. As long as there's appropriate cover at design level, and the construction quality's consistent, then there shouldn't be a problem.

Loreta: Isn't inadequate cover more of a problem in a slender structure, though? You'd probably have less cover, compared with the big lumps of concrete they use for coastal defences.

Mike: Not if …

Hanif: Just a second.

Mike: Yes, Hanif?

Hanif: Let's just think about what we're trying to resolve, here. The key issue is, what's the most suitable long-term solution? And in both cases, we're saying steel is necessary, either in an all-steel tubular structure or in the form of reinforcement inside concrete. But obviously exposed steel is unsuitable because of the problem of corrosion. So the question is, what's the most reliable way of protecting steel, over the long term? And we have to bear in mind that, just because something requires regular maintenance, such as painting, that doesn't necessarily mean it's unreliable. As long as the maintenance is consistent. The key question is, what's the most economical approach? So painting a steel structure every couple of years is uneconomical only if the cost of painting is more expensive than the additional cost of using concrete at the time of construction.

Mike: So, to determine the most efficient solution, we need to assess the lifespan of a reinforced concrete structure. If we know that, we can determine how many times the equivalent steel structure would need to be repainted over that same period, and what the cost of that would be.

Hanif: Yeah.

Mike: But this is really the point I'm making, Hanif. We can't categorically say that reinforced concrete is inefficient unless we look into it in detail.

Hanif: Of course not. Look, let me make a suggestion …

▬ 10.2

Su: With very tall structures, one of the main loads you need to take into consideration, clearly, is the mass of the structure, its weight. Due to gravity, that mass exerts a downward load, which has to be transmitted to the ground. So that downward force means the structure is in compression, especially near the bottom. Obviously, the closer you are to the bottom, the more compressive force the structure is subjected to. But with tall structures, downward load compressing the structural elements is only part of the problem. Another major force acting on the structure is wind load, which is a horizontal load, exerted by air pressure against one side of the structure. Because the structure is fixed at ground level, and free at the top, that generates bending forces. And when elements bend, you have opposing forces: compression at one side, tension at the other. And at ground level, the wind effectively tries to slide the structure along the ground, and the foundations below the ground resist that. The result of that is shear force between the substructure and the superstructure. The wind generates tensile loads on the foundations of tall structures as well, as the bending action tries to pull them out of the ground on one side, a bit like a tree being uprooted by the wind. So the foundations need to rely on friction with the ground to resist the pull-out force, just as tree roots do. The action of the wind can also generate torsion. You get a twisting force sometimes, when the air pressure is comparatively higher against one corner of a building, although that's less of a problem with chimneys because of their circular profile. With very large masses of concrete, you also have to think about the forces generated by thermal movement. When concrete absorbs heat from the sun, you get expansion; as soon as the sun goes in, there's contraction. That movement can be significant over a large area, especially as the sun generally heats one side of a structure much more than the other. So there are all kinds of different forces acting on a tall structure.

▭ 10.3

Andrej: The record speed exceeded the standard operating speed by a huge margin. It was 80% faster at its peak. So you would imagine that the TGV used for the record run was heavily modified. In fact, that wasn't really the case. The train was modified to a certain extent but, with a few exceptions, it was essentially just an ordinary TGV. As you can see from this slide, one of the biggest differences was that the modified train was significantly shorter, in order to make it lighter. There was a 50% reduction in length, down to 100 metres, compared with a 200-metre standard length. The coaches being pulled were perfectly standard – the only differences were that some of the seats had been removed to make way for all of the monitoring equipment that was carried on board. And some changes were made to the bodywork, to make it slightly more aerodynamic, which meant the drag coefficient was reduced by 15%. The wheels on the modified train were marginally bigger than the standard size. The diameter was increased by 19%, in order to reduce the speed of revolution, to limit friction and centrifugal force. And the power of the electric motors was substantially higher than the standard units – boosted by 68%. But none of the changes was fundamental. So my point is, standard high-speed trains can be made to go faster by a considerable amount.

▭ 10.4

Narrator: In the late 1940s and early '50s, the United States Air Force carried out a series of experiments to explore how much physical stress the human body could withstand. A key aim was to test how much G-force pilots were able to cope with and see what would happen if they exceeded their limits. Led by Air Force doctor John Paul Stapp, a number of spectacular tests were carried out at Edwards Air Force Base in California, a location suitable for the experiments thanks to its 600-metre rail track, specially designed for high-speed rocket tests. A rocket sled, capable of reaching speeds approaching the sound barrier, was mounted on the track. On top of the sled, named *Sonic Wind*, researchers fixed a seat, intended for an abnormally brave volunteer. Refusing to give the dangerous job to a member of his team, the man in the hot seat was John Stapp himself. Over several runs, Stapp was subjected to progressively greater extremes of force. Each time, he resisted. Eventually, the time came to take the ultimate risk, to surpass what many doctors believed to be a deadly level of G-force. And so on December 10th 1954, Stapp was strapped onto *Sonic Wind* for the mother of all rides.

▭ 10.5

Narrator: That day, Stapp was subjected to extremes of force beyond the imagination. When the sled's rockets fired, he shot from zero to over 1,000 kilometres per hour in just three seconds, subjecting him to 20 Gs. When the sled hit the pool of water in the braking zone, it was like hitting a brick wall. Stapp slowed from the speed of a bullet to a complete stop in little more than a single second. Incredibly, John Stapp survived the ride, although so much blood had rushed into his eyes that he was unable to see for some time afterwards. Before the test, doctors had believed that human beings were incapable of surviving forces greater than 17 Gs. When the sled hit the water, Stapp had pulled a crushing 46 Gs.

▭ 10.6

Jasmine: I think what he's suggesting in terms of acceleration and deceleration forces is reasonable.

Andrew: Yeah. 2 G sounds about right. Anything less than that, and the track length's going to exceed the size of the site. And if you start getting close to 3 G, or beyond that, then that's probably going to be a bit too much for the average passenger.

Jasmine: I'd say so. His calculations for the total distance for acceleration and deceleration seem about right. The problem I have is with the length of the track. I think his ten-kilometre figure is OK for an ideal world scenario, but it doesn't leave much margin for error.

Andrew: No. Because at full speed, you're going to be covering, what, a kilometre every three seconds. So if there's some kind of problem, you're going to be eating up the kilometres at a pretty frightening rate.

Jasmine: You can say that again. I think he'll need every kilometre of track length he can get on that site. Plus some sort of emergency stopping facility at the end of the line, just in case.

Andrew: Definitely, yeah.

Jasmine: Then I don't know what you think about using wheels, instead of skids.

Andrew: Well, technically, it's feasible to build wheels capable of spinning at that sort of speed, because it's been done on land speed record cars. The only problem is, if you get a wheel failure at the kind of speeds we're talking about, the consequences are going to be unthinkable.

Jasmine: Yeah. I haven't calculated exactly what centrifugal forces they'd have to cope with, but for wheels of about 500 mil diameter, at full speed, I worked out they'd be spinning at over 13,000 rpm.

Andrew: Yeah, that's a lot. Plus, of course, skids should give better frictional resistance under braking.

Jasmine: Possibly.

Andrew: Maybe not?

Jasmine: Well, the friction from wheel bearings spinning at that sort of speed might be higher. And the skids wouldn't be in permanent contact with the rails, don't forget. But, anyway, I think skids are the only safe option.

Andrew: I'd go for skids. Definitely.

Jasmine: And then for the brakes, I think the first point is that, for the initial deceleration, even without applying any brakes, the aerodynamic resistance is going to be huge. In fact, that alone might even exceed 2 G, for a short time.

Andrew: Possibly. It'd depend how much drag there was, which obviously depends on the bodywork design, doesn't it?

Jasmine: Yeah.

Andrew: I don't like the idea of a friction system, against the rails. It would have to withstand a tremendous amount of heat.

Jasmine: Yeah. I think that's a non-starter, at these kinds of speeds. Aerodynamic braking has got to be the best option. Possibly, you could deploy flaps initially, at top speed, then maybe release a parachute as a second stage. Maybe deploy the parachute at, I don't know, what sort of speeds do dragsters reach? They use parachutes, don't they? What do they do? 400 Ks?

Andrew: A bit more, I think. 450, something like that. There's also the option of reverse engine thrust, like they use on aircraft.

Jasmine: In that case, though, you'd still need another system, in case you get an engine failure. But it's a possibility. I think the bottom line is that it needs a combination of systems to make it absolutely fail-safe.

ANSWER KEY

Unit 1

2a
1 navigation
2 (monitoring) delivery vehicles
3 (finding) stolen cars
4 drift
5 man overboard
6 innovative uses of

b
1 uses
2 use
3 user's; useful

3a
2 d 3 b 4 f 5 a 6 e

4a
1 allows
2 prevents
3 ensures; enables

b
1 ensures
2 allows / enables
3 prevents

c
1 allow/enable
2 allow/enable
3 ensure
4 allow/enable
5 prevent

6a
See text in Exercise 6b on page 8

c
2 i 3 a 4 b 5 g 6 h 7 c
8 d 9 f

7a
2 support
3 attached
4 raised
5 power
6 ascend
7 transport

c
The notes are missing articles (a/an, the) and some auxiliary verbs (e.g. be).

8a
See audioscript 1.3 on page 86

b
1 By a floating structure
2 To attach the base to the seabed
3 Ships would carry them
4 Collisions between the cable and space debris
5 The anchors would be raised and the station would be moved.

9a
Suggested answer
The anchoring system
The wind loads on the cable will be huge. What are the implications for the anchoring system? The base will need to be moved continually and sometimes urgently. What temporary system could be used to hold the base in position? Should the base be in shallow water near the coast, or in deep water further offshore? The choice will have an impact on the design of the anchor system.

The propulsion system
Will the weight of the cable allow the base to be moved by its own propellers or will a more powerful system for propulsion and control be required? For example, an external power source.

b
Suggested answers
Anchor system
It will be possible to anchor the base more securely in shallow water, near the coast. A permanent anchor structure could be built on the ocean bed, in shallow water. The base station could then be fixed securely to it with cables. If several anchor structures are built at different locations along the coast, the base station can be moved between them.
Propulsion system
Tugs (powerful boats used for pulling ships) could be used as an external power source. However, the base station could be driven by its own propellers. The large, powerful engines needed to propel it would be heavy, but that isn't necessarily a disadvantage, as extra mass, and therefore extra inertia, would help to make the base more stable.

10
A technical advantage is a type of technology that is superior in some way – for example, more efficient, more powerful or more reliable – compared with a related type of technology – for example, a competing product (one sold by another company) – or compared with an earlier model of the same product.

11a
It's a flat belt for lifting elevators which is used instead of a cable. Compared with cables, the Gen2 system has a number of advantages.

b
2 e 3 b 4 f 5 c 6 a

c
2 reduces
3 conventional
4 reduce
5 enhance
6 conventional
7 superior
8 eliminates

12a
1 enhanced
2 reduced
3 eliminated
4 conventional
5 superior

b
1 c 2 b 3 a 4 d

c
2 dramatically
3 entirely
4 extremely
5 considerably
6 highly
7 exceptionally
8 significantly

d
1 entirely; totally
2 considerably; dramatically
3 exceptionally; highly

14a
1 That you shouldn't use jargon or it will sound like nonsense and that technical concepts can be difficult to explain, even using everyday language.
2 Explanations that are boring.
3 Speaking to an adult as if you're talking to a child.

c
Richard suggests using everyday language to avoid explanations not being understood; using some jargon and then explaining it using everyday language to avoid sounding patronising; explaining difficult concepts by comparing technical points with things in everyday life to illustrate them; and using some humour to avoid sounding dull.

15b
2 A column going down into the ground
3 To drill
4 Concrete poured on the construction site in its final position
5 Made at a factory, away from the site
6 To hammer in
7 Like a giant hammer
8 Like a giant drill
9 A kind of clay suspension / a sort of mud

d
1 put simply; in other words; basically
2 effectively; essentially; basically
3 what we call; what we refer to as
4 if you imagine; if you picture

16
Suggested answers
There are two types of pile foundation: end-bearing piles and friction piles. Essentially, end-bearing piles are used when you have soft ground which is on top of hard ground or rock. Basically, the piles go through the soft ground and sit on the hard ground below. It's a bit like building over water. The soft ground is like water, which can't support anything, and the hard ground below it is like the seabed. Put simply, the piles are like stilts. Friction piles are different. They're used when there's no hard ground. In simple terms, the sides of the pile grip the soft ground around them. If you picture a nail in a piece of wood, it's the same thing. The nail is gripped by the wood around it. Sometimes the bottoms of friction piles are made wider. Imagine a leg with a foot at the bottom, it's the same principle.

Unit 2

2a
2 Glass
3 Copper
4 Aluminium
5 Timber
6 Rubber
7 Plastic

b
2 a 3 b 4 f 5 d 6 h
7 e 8 g

c
2 with
3 from
4 from
5 with
6 of
7 of
8 from

3b
The main point that Irina makes is that it's important to consider the total environmental impact of a product, including producing it (pre-use), using it (in-use) and recycling it (post-use). She gives the example of an energy-saving light bulb.

c

Sophia and Pete's ideas:

Pre-use: aluminium production (extraction from ore and recycling), coating steel (galvanising), transporting and handling bulk material, cutting and welding

In-use: weight (impact on fuel consumption), lifespan (frequency of manufacturing)

d

Suggested answers

Electrical wires in vehicles

For pre-use, as far as I know, it takes more energy to produce aluminium than to produce copper, if it's derived from ore. However, it takes less energy to transport aluminium, because it's lighter.

For in-use, I'm sure aluminium is better because it's lighter, so the vehicle would consume less fuel.

For post-use, both aluminium and copper can be recycled. I'd say it takes less energy to handle and transport aluminium, because it's lighter.

External walls in houses

For pre-use, it takes a lot of energy to produce bricks because they have to be fired in a kiln. They're also heavy to transport. Softwood is lighter to transport, and I'd say it probably takes less energy to saw it and handle it, compared with making bricks. During construction, building with bricks uses more energy, as sand and cement have to be transported and mixed to make mortar.

For in-use, wood is a better insulator than brick which is an advantage, as the house should take less energy to heat. In theory, softwood could last as long as bricks, if it's properly maintained. But in practice, that will often not be the case. So, construction energy could sometimes be higher for softwood, as houses need to be rebuilt more often.

For post-use, it's possible to recover both bricks and softwood for re-use, but neither is very easy to recycle.

4

Suggested answers

1   Brakes are designed to slow down vehicles or moving parts. Often they work through friction, by applying pressure to pads which are pressed against the sides of a disc, the inside of a drum, or directly against a wheel rim. Alternatives include systems that use electromagnetic force, systems that exploit the braking effects of engines or flywheels (via clutches and gearboxes), aerodynamic braking systems (for example spoilers on aircraft, parachutes on dragsters), and reverse thrusters on jet engines. Brake discs are often made of ferrous metals (iron-based – for example steel), or sometimes ceramic materials.

2   Examples of materials used to make pads include: compounds of advanced materials (cars), ferrous metals (trains), rubber (bicycles), ceramics (performance cars).

5a

Green refers to ecological issues. Red refers to heat (*red hot* means very hot). Also, a *hot topic* is a current important topic.

b

1   Because they use friction, which wastes energy as heat

2   They recover heat and use it to power the car.

3   The ability to generate high levels of friction, and to resist the effects of friction and consequent heat

4   Heat from the engine being absorbed by the chassis, which can damage sensitive parts such as electronic components and plastic parts

c

2 g   3 b   4 f   5 d   6 a   7 e

6c

1 c   2 b   3 d   4 a   5 e

e

1   b; c   4   e
2   d; e   5   a; b; c
3   d

8c

2   abrasion resistance
3   thermal stability
4   durable
5   lightweight

9a

1 c   2 e   3 b   4 a   5 d

b

1   tyres   4   bullet-resistant armour
2   drive belts   5   sealing gaskets
3   brake pads

c

Suggested answers

In tyres, puncture and tear resistance help to stop punctures and blowouts and abrasion resistance helps the tyre to last longer. In drive belts, high elasticity allows belts to fit tightly and abrasion resistance helps them resist the friction caused by the belt turning. In brake pads, abrasion resistance helps the pads to last longer and thermal stability helps them resist the heat generated during braking. Kevlar® helps make bullet-resistant armour, which is generally heavy, more lightweight, which is better for the vehicle's performance. Kevlar® makes sealing gaskets durable and its thermal stability allows them to resist heat – for example, in engine cylinder heads – and its chemical stability means gaskets are not affected by engine fluids such as fuel, lubricating oil and coolant liquids.

10a

1   At the dentist's
2   The tool is a dental drill.
3   Titanium can be used for the handle, and tungsten-carbide and diamond for the bur.

b

1   lightweight   3   durable
2   abrasion resistance   4   thermal stability

c

1 b   2 a   3 e   4 c   5 d

12

Suggested answers

1   Examples of situations used in advertising include motor racing, water sports such as surfing and diving, and aviation.

2   The intended message is that watches are accurate and are resistant.

3   Higher quality watches keep good time; are resistant to water and shocks; and are made from more expensive, better-looking materials.

4   Describing something as water-resistant suggests it can resist water up to a certain limit, for example to a certain depth or pressure. Describing something as waterproof suggests it gives unlimited protection from water.

13a

1   corrosion resistance
2   water resistance
3   scratch resistance
4   shock resistance

14a

1   Watch materials are sometimes chosen for marketing reasons, not technical reasons.

2   They considered using submarine-grade steel in some models even though water resistance actually depends on the joints and seals, not the metal used.

3   Many good watch-making materials are either ordinary, or complex, and so are not very marketable.

4   Consumers are not technical experts, and make choices based on their impressions, rather than on factual information.

b

1   T
2   T
3   F – it needs a protective coating.
4   F – he says it's fairly poor in terms of looks.
5   F – no – for the reasons given above.
6   F – inadequate materials have never been chosen for marketing reasons.
7   T
8   F – complicated names are not good for marketing.

c

2   exceptionally resistant
3   not at all suitable
4   tremendously marketable
5   relatively complex
6   not all that good

d

1   extremely, exceptionally, tremendously
2   quite, fairly, pretty, relatively
3   not very, not particularly, not (all) that
4   not enough, insufficiently, not adequately
5   definitely not, not at all

15

Suggested answers

Steel is relatively heavy and very tough. It is pretty scratch-resistant and shock-resistant. Mild steel is not very corrosion-resistant but stainless steel has good corrosion resistance and is therefore suitable for watches. Glass is quite heavy and is water-resistant and corrosion-resistant. Ordinary glass is very brittle and has fairly poor shock resistance and scratch resistance, although it is still suitable for watches. Toughened glass is more durable. Aluminium is relatively lightweight and is fairly tough. It has good corrosion resistance. It is therefore suitable for watches. Titanium is exceptionally lightweight and tough and has excellent abrasion resistance. It is also extremely corrosion-resistant and is therefore an excellent watch material. Gold is extremely heavy and pretty tough, although softer grades of gold have quite poor shock resistance and scratch resistance. Gold has excellent corrosion resistance. It is suitable for more expensive, decorative watches.

Unit 3

2a

The aim of the project is to formulate a policy that will state which plug and socket configurations their company recommends, and explain the technical reasons why they are recommended.

b

The *profile of the pins* means the shape of the individual pins, for example a rectangular cross-section or a circular cross-section.

A *standard configuration* means a uniform arrangement, for example in a given country all plugs have a standard layout – they all exactly the same.

c

a 6   b 4   c 1   d 5   e 2
f 3

d

2 rounded   5 linear
3 rectangular   6 triangular
4 cylindrical

e

rectangle; rectangular; triangle; triangular; cylinder; cylindrical; line; linear

3a

Picture b

b

2 ridges; grooves; recessed; flush with; set back
3 pins

4a

1 Advantages: The plug resists pullout forces. Nothing can touch the pins if the plug is partially pulled out.
   Disadvantages: It's difficult to pull out.
2 Advantages: Children can't stick things in the socket.
   Disadvantages: If the mechanism is too sensitive, it can be difficult to insert the plug.

5

See audioscript 3.6 on page 88

6a

1 T
2 F – casting is a different discipline
3 F – it's a slang term
4 F – work involving abrasives is noisier
5 T
6 T

b

1 Sawing   4 Milling
2 Shearing   5 Flame-cutting
3 Drilling

c

2 guillotine   5 abrasive wheel
3 kerf   6 hole-saw
4 toothed blade

7a

secondary operations: additional machining, such as polishing
net-shaped parts: parts with accurately cut edges; often intricate shapes
heat-affected zone: the area modified by high temperatures (resulting from the heat of cutting)
mechanical stresses: physical forces such as shear forces when sawing or guillotining metal
narrow kerf: narrow thickness of material removed during cutting; especially easy to do with waterjet cutting
tightly nested: when several components are cut from the same piece of material the components can be placed close together, making better use of the material.

b

1 net-shaped parts
2 heat-affected zone
3 mechanical stresses
4 narrow kerf

c

1 especially good when
2 useless when
3 not the best solution
4 ideal for

8

Suggested answers

Drilling with a bit is good for cutting blind holes.
Drilling with a hole-saw is ideal for cutting timber.
Flame-cutting is perfect for cutting metals. It's useless for cutting ceramics.
Grinding is perfect for cutting wide kerfs. It's totally unsuitable if you don't want a heat-affected zone.
Guillotining is especially good for cutting thin materials. It's not particularly suitable for cutting thick materials.
Milling is especially good for cutting metals. It's totally unsuitable for cutting timber.
Punching is suitable for cutting through holes. It's useless for cutting blind holes.
Sawing is ideal for cutting straight edges. It's not so good if you need to cut curved edges.
Water jet cutting is ideal if you need curved edges. It's not so good for cutting very thick materials.

9

See audioscript 3.8 on page 88

10a

1 To involve their suppliers more actively in design
2 Doing a lot of work for no return and covering costs
3 They want to work with fewer suppliers, so there would be more work.

b

1 Mechanical fixings: screw, rivet, clip
2 Non-mechanical fixings: weld, adhesive

c

1 weld   4 screw
2 bolt   5 rivet
3 adhesive   6 clip

d

1 joining; fixing
2 bolting; riveting
3 bonding; welding; gluing

11a

1 together
2 each other
3 on
4 to/onto

b

1 on   4 onto/to
2 each other   5 to
3 together

c

1 Main advantage: They can be removed easily.
   Main disadvantage: They can work loose.
2 It can't be removed easily.
3 Fixings can be inadequately tightened. Adhesives can be used on improperly prepared surfaces. Welds can be flawed.

12a

Suggested answers

1 In early aircraft, timber frames were joined together with adhesive / glued together, or screws / screwed together.
2 In jet aircraft, alloy body panels are joined together with rivets / riveted together.
3 In aircraft cabins, the seats are fixed to the floor with bolts / bolted to the floor.

4 In aircraft cockpits, the windshield is bonded to the fuselage with adhesive / glued to the fuselage.

13a

See article on page 28

b

a 2   b 3   c 4   d 1

c

a The balloons climbed faster than expected, then entered controlled airspace adjacent to an airport.
b A rope tangled with a power line, then Mr Walters was arrested.
c The modern equivalent, cluster ballooning, is not a mainstream sport, but is becoming more popular.
d A garden chair, helium-filled weather balloons and ropes

14a

a over
b below; beneath; underneath
c alongside; adjacent to; beside
d around
e outside
f inside; within

b

1 above   4 within
2 around   5 beneath
3 in

c

2 inserted   5 located
3 situated   6 projecting
4 suspended   7 positioned

d

located; situated

15a

See audioscript 3.9 on page 88

b

1 It's pretty time-consuming to assemble.
2 Cable ties are fastened around the bottoms of the balloons, to fix them to the ropes.
3 The balloons are attached to ropes of different lengths, which are attached in groups to straps, like the branches of a tree.
4 Water is carried in bags, as ballast. Taps on the bags are used to release water.
5 The balloons can be released one by one.
6 The balloons can't be released one by one.

c

Suggested answers

The helium could be contained within a smaller number of larger balloons. The balloons could be made of stronger material than weather balloons, and could be permanently fastened to the ropes or straps. This would make the balloon cluster faster to put together and inflate. Two or three of the balloons could have valves, allowing helium to be released during the flight. This would also allow the balloons to be deflated after the flight, so that they could be reused.

Unit 4

1

For the design of a large cruise ship, several hundred drawings would need to be produced. These would include general arrangement drawings, such as plans of the overall layout of each deck, elevations of the sides of the ship, and cross-sections through the ship at different points. Notes on these general arrangement drawings would then refer to more detailed drawings of assembly details. As well as being divided into small-scale general arrangement drawings and larger-scale details, the drawings would also be organised into different specialisations, such as structure, electrical power circuits, lighting circuits, water supply, air-conditioning, lifts, fire sprinkler systems, engine installations, etc.

2a
1   Part of a staircase (Staircase 3, Deck C)
2   The number of panels, and their size

b
2   elevation
3   exploded view
4   cross-section
5   schematic
6   note
7   specification

c
general arrangement: plan, elevation
detail: exploded view, cross-section

d
1   elevation   4   schematic
2   cross-section   5   exploded view
3   plan

3a
The scale is the ratio between the size of items shown on a drawing, and their actual size (in reality). A scale rule has several scales, allowing dimensions to be measured on a drawing, to determine the actual size.

b
1   The width of the panel at the top.
2   That you shouldn't scale off drawings. It's mentioned because Pavel suggests measuring the dimension on the drawings with a scale rule to find out the actual dimensions.

c
1   *Is this drawing to scale?* = Do the dimensions correspond with a scale?
2   *It's one to five.* = The dimensions on the drawing are 1/5 of their real size.
3   *... you shouldn't scale off drawings ...* = You shouldn't measure dimensions on a drawing using a scale rule and take them to be exact.
4   *... it's actual size, on a full-scale drawing ...* = The dimensions on the drawing are the same as their real size.

4
Types of drawing required: a plan showing the perimeter of the handrail (possible scale 1:100); an elevation of a short length of the handrail (possible scale 1:10); a section of the handrail (possible scale 1:10); details showing key connections, such as those between handrail posts and deck, and top rail and posts (possible scale – actual size). Specification: type of steel, types of welded joint, types of bolt, type and colour of paint/coating, other materials such as plastic surround to top rail

6a
The words mean how exact something is, for example how closely the sizes of manufactured items match their designed size.

b
1   A superflat floor has a much flatter surface. It's finished more precisely than an ordinary concrete floor.
2   Ordinary slabs can be flat to +/– 5mm. Superflat slabs can be flat to within 1mm.
3   Slight variations in floor level can cause forklifts to tilt, causing the forks to hit racks or drop items.

c
Tolerance is the acceptable difference between ideal designed size and actual size. In machining and assembly processes, it is impossible to achieve entirely precise sizes. A degree of tolerance is always required.

d
1   within
2   plus; minus
3   tight
4   outside

e
1   outside tolerance
2   +/– 0.5mm
3   within tolerance
4   tight tolerance

f
Difference in meaning: Plus or minus 1mm means the size may vary by a maximum of 1 mm either side of the 'ideal' dimension. As an example, if the diameter of a steel bar is specified as 100 mm +/– 1 mm, the diameter may be a maximum of 101 mm at its widest point and 99 mm at its narrowest point. Since the total variation can be 1 mm either side of the 100 mm 'ideal' (between 99 mm and 101 mm), the maximum total variation between the widest and narrowest points is 2 mm. However, no point must be further than 1 mm either side of the 'ideal' size.
Within 1 mm describes only the total variation in size. This means the size may vary by a maximum of 1mm above the ideal dimension (as long as no point is below the ideal dimension) or it may vary by a maximum of 1mm below the ideal dimension (as long as no point is above the ideal dimension). Therefore, a minimum diameter of 100 and a maximum of 101 would be within 1 mm, as would a minimum of 99 and a maximum of 100, and a minimum of 99.5 and a maximum of 100.5.
Examples of uses: It is usual to specify +/– tolerances where a specific ideal size is critical, for example the size of a hole for a bolt. In this case, if the hole is too narrow (too far below the ideal size) the bolt will not fit into it. If the hole is too wide (too far above the ideal size), the bolt will not fit tightly enough. 'Within' is often used when specifying tolerances for concrete floor surfaces. In this case, the important issue is the total amount of variation between the highest and lowest points on the surface of the floor (which determines how smooth the floor is).

7a
1   A superflat finish for the entire floor
2   Free movement floors are superflat everywhere. On defined movement floors, only specific lanes are superflat.
3   Long, narrow lanes allow a higher-quality finish to be achieved.
4   This can be done at a later stage to make other parts of the floor superflat.
5   It can be positioned deeper in the concrete.

b
1   long   4   thick
2   wide   5   depth
3   height

c
2   width   5   thickness
3   length   6   height
4   depth

d
diameter: the maximum width of a circle
radius: the distance from the centre of a circle to its circumference (half the diameter)

8
The capital T refers to the thickness of the flanges. The small t refers to the thickness of the web. The capital W refers to the width of the flanges. The small w refers to half the width of the column from the centre of the web to the edges of the flanges. The small r refers to the radius of the curve at the joint between the web and the flanges. The capital D refers to the total depth of the column, from the top of one flange to the bottom of the opposite flange. The small d refers to the depth of the web, measured between the ends of the curves at the joints, at the point where the curves are flush with the face of the web.

9
A design process is the development of a design. A typical design starts with a design brief, which states the design objectives. Initial ideas are then put together as rough sketches. These are then developed into preliminary drawings, which are more detailed and are often drawn to scale. The preliminary drawings are then developed, incorporating comments from different members of the design team, consultants and the client. Once the design has been sufficiently developed, working drawings are produced. These are then used for manufacturing/assembly/construction. Frequently, working drawings are revised (changed) during this latter phase, in order to resolve technical problems encountered during manufacturing/assembly/construction.

10a
1   design information (at different stages of the design process)
2   sketches, design brief, revised/amended drawing, superseded drawing, preliminary drawing, working drawing, summary/notes

b
1 b   2 d   3 c   4 a   5 e

c
1   sketch   3   working drawing
2   design brief   4   preliminary drawing

d
2   revise   6   supersede
3   rough   7   specify
4   issue   8   resolve
5   comment on

e
Suggested answers
1   The drawing needs to be amended/revised.
2   The design needs to be sent to the client for comments and approval.
3   The site engineer needs to be contacted to check which revision of the drawing they have.
4   The three different contractors need to be issued with the revision.
5   Rough sketches need to be done first and the client to comment on them.

11b
1 b   2 a   3 c

d
1   The senior engineer will decide whether or not the team needs further revisions of a drawing.
2   If the drawing is needed, the team will receive copies of all further revisions. If not, no further revisions will be issued to the team.
3   S/he will liaise between the mechanical and electrical teams, and will report to the project manager.
4   All three design teams will be located in a single open-plan office.

e

Suggested answers

1 First, the preliminary drawing will be circulated to all the senior engineers. The engineers will decide whether or not the drawing is required by their team. If not, they will say it isn't required and after that, no more revisions of the drawing will be issued to them. If the drawing is required, they'll say it's needed. They might comment on the drawing and request amendments or approve it. They will also receive all further revisions of the drawing, including working drawings.

2 The mechanical and electrical teams will be able to work on the preliminary design together easily, thanks to the open-plan office. As the drawings are developed they'll be able to discuss amendments in the same way.

3 The mechanical and structural teams will be able to work together to solve the problem in the open-plan office and revised drawings will be produced. These will then be approved by both the mechanical and structural teams. Revised drawings will be issued and circulated to all those who need them.

12

Often conflicting (different) information is shown on different drawings. On one drawing, the dimensions of a component may not correspond with those shown on a related drawing. Clashes are another common problem – different drawings may show different components in the same position within an assembly, meaning the assembly will not fit together as designed. Key dimensions and assembly details may also be missing from the set of drawings, leaving the production with inadequate information.

13a

1 Design problems and solutions

2 A query is a question. An instruction is an explanation of what to do / official permission to do something.

3 Written follow-up is important in order to keep a record for contractual/financial purposes.

b

2 869   4 867; 868
3 869; 870   5 867; 868; 869

c

1 clash   4 advise
2 request   5 clarify
3 propose

14a

See audioscript 4.6 on page 89

b

2 clarify   6 alternative
3 contradicts   7 as per
4 clash   8 confirm
5 propose

d

Suggested answers

As discussed today, I confirm that the connection between the plate and T section on the ski lift should have six bolts, not eight as shown on the detail. The two bolts shown on the detail which would clash with the flange of the T section are not required.

![Unit 5]

Unit 5

1

See audioscript 5.1 on page 89

2a

1 To finish first, first you must finish
2 Engineering enemies
3 Wear and tear

b

1 heat   4 shocks
2 pressure   5 abrasion
3 vibration

c

Suggested answers

1 shocks
2 heat
3 abrasion
4 shocks
5 abrasion
6 abrasion
7 shocks
8 pressure (caused by heat)
9 vibration

3a

1 T
2 F – the driver switched the engine off
3 T
4 T
5 F – the wheel nut wouldn't turn
6 F – the driver didn't bend the suspension

b

1 blocking   3 bend; snap
2 jam   4 crack

c

1 leaking out   4 clog up
2 run out   5 wearing out
3 cut out   6 blow up

d

See audioscript 5.2 on page 89

e

2 leaking out   6 blocked (up)
3 jammed   7 bent
4 clogged up   8 worn out
5 worked loose   9 run out

4

Monza has long straights and several chicanes. This means cars are at full-throttle for longer, and need to do a lot of heavy braking. Problems: Engines can overheat and blow up; brakes can overheat; riding the kerbs can cause the suspension to crack, bend or snap; the right-hand corners cause the tyres on the left of the car to wear out faster than those on the right side; and leaves can block up the radiators.

5b

User's observations = what the person using the machine has noticed
Nature of fault = type of problem
Circumstances of fault = in what type of situation the fault happened/happens
External factors = things from outside, for example the weather or something hitting the machine
Process of elimination = thinking of possible problems and deciding which are *not* possible in order to reduce the number of possibilities
Identify the fault = find the fault / decide what the fault is
Determine action and urgency = decide what to do about the problem and decide how quickly it needs to be done

---

6a

1 Check injection
2 Water in the fuel system
3 Because the fuel was put in directly from a delivery tanker
4 When the engine is started from cold
5 A faulty fuel pre-heater plug
6 The plug can be changed at the next service. It's not an urgent problem.

b

1 defect   5 properly
2 defective; faulty 6 intermittently
3 major   7 systematically
4 minor

c

1 b   2 c   3 a

d

Suggested answers

1 This is an intermittent problem. It's probably caused by wear and tear.
2 This was a sudden problem. It's probably a faulty part, or an installation problem.
3 This is a systematic problem. It's probably a faulty part, or an installation problem.

e

2 It sounds like it's
3 It could be / It might be
4 I doubt it's
5 It can't be

f

2 it might be   5 I doubt it's
3 it might be   6 It sounds like it's
4 it can't be

7a

minor; systematic

b

Suggested answers

It can't be water in the fuel supply. (This would cause misfiring.)
It could be a clogged fuel filter. (The engine is performing consistently, but is down on power.)
I doubt it's a compression leak. (This would probably result in increased fuel consumption, and would probably cause more major problems.)
It can't be a lubrication problem. (This would cause overheating.)
I doubt it's a blockage in the exhaust system. (This would cause more major problems.)

8

checklists = lists of things to be checked
standard procedures = specific, planned ways of dealing with situations and problems
back-up installations = secondary/additional equipment that will work if main equipment fails
planned maintenance = replacing parts at planned times even if they are not worn out

9a

1 An incorrect (oversized) hydraulic pipe was fitted to the right-hand engine.
2 The pipe rubbed against a fuel line.
3 The fuel line ruptured, resulting in a major leak.

b

04:58 b   05:36 d   06:13 a
06:27 c

c

2 oversized   7 disproportionate
3 inadequate   8 irregular
4 undetected   9 imbalance
5 abnormal   10 malfunction
6 insufficient   11 inoperable

d
1 incorrect/abnormal
2 inadequate/insufficient
3 irregular
4 oversized
5 malfunction
6 imbalance
7 undetected
8 inoperable

10a
1 F – the tyre pressures are well down
2 T
3 F – only one group of tyres is low
4 T

b
1 abnormal/incorrect
2 insufficient/inadequate
3 disproportionate
4 proportionate

c
In general, insufficient tyre pressures could be caused by: pressure loss over time (all tyres lose air pressure progressively over a period of several months) due to inadequate maintenance; a slow puncture (air leaking slowly from a small hole in the tyre); air leaking from a valve due to a problem with the valve, for example dirt in the valve preventing it from closing properly; a faulty pressure gauge on the compressor used to inflate the tyres, giving an incorrect pressure reading. With this specific problem, perhaps there was a fault with the compressor used to inflate that block of tyres − a different compressor to the one used to inflate the other blocks − and this gave the maintenance technician an incorrect pressure reading when inflating that block of tyres. It's unlikely that a technical problem with the tyres, such as slow punctures or leaking valves, would occur on several tyres at the same time and cause exactly the same loss in pressure across all the tyres.

11a
Suggested answers
Repairs are done to correct technical problems after breakdowns have occurred.
Maintenance is done to prevent technical problems from occurring.

broken = repair, for example a bolt that has broken
clogged = repair, for example a filter that is completely clogged and has caused a technical problem, or maintenance it is slightly clogged and is ready to be replaced
defective = repair, for example a part that was incorrectly manufactured and did not work
faulty = repair, for example a sensor that is giving incorrect measurements
worn = maintenance, for example worn tyres need to be replaced

b
Suggested answers
Similarities: parts and fluids are replaced on a planned maintenance programme, parts are checked visually for wear and damage, and that they are tightly fixed, correctly aligned/balanced, etc.
Main difference: standards in aviation are more rigorous

12a

2 d	3 c	4 a	5 g	6 b
7 j	8 e	9 h	10 i	

b

2 d	3 j	4 g	5 c	6 b
7 i	8 a	9 h	10 e	

13a
1 The level is OK.
2 The coolant is full of residue / black.
3 It looks reasonable.
4 OK, there are no signs of damage.
5 This will need to be looked at.

b
They're working on an industrial machine as their decision not to change the filter would be unacceptable in aircraft maintenance.

c
Drain the coolant. Remove the filter, examine it and clean it. Put the filter back in. Replace the coolant. Adjust the blades and tighten them.

14a
A forklift truck hit a machine unit IPS15 and made a hole in the main panel. The technician at the factory looked at the machine (he did not open it up or look inside) and reported that the blade alignment mechanism was damaged and that liquid lubricant was leaking from the unit. There was also an electrical crackling sound (presumably caused by earthing/short-circuiting) when the machine was switched on.

b
Isolate the electrical supply. Dismantle the external panels. Drain the lubricant. Check for internal damage. Remove damaged parts and replace them. Add lubricant. Adjust the blades. Put on the external panels. Reconnect the electrical supply. Test the machine.

■■■ Unit 6

1
Needs analysis (also called requirement analysis / gap analysis) is finding out what the requirements are for a new project by looking at all the factors that are involved and how they will interact.
Budget = how much money is available, for example the budget for designing, building and testing a prototype for a new high-speed train
Capacity = how much something needs to produce or carry, for example how much power an electrical circuit must be able to carry
Dimensions = size, for example the diameter of the wheels of a mountain bike
Layout = the overall shape of something and the positions of different parts relative to one another, for example the layout of the main components of a car engine.
Looks = what something looks like from an aesthetic point of view, for example the look of a car in terms of the shape of its bodywork
Performance = similar to capacity, for example how much power a generator needs to produce
Regulations = laws and standards that a design must comply with, for example safety regulations and quality standards
Timescale = how much time is available, for example the schedule for building a new airport

2a

1 capacity	3 timescale
2 graphics	

b
1 regard
2 terms
3 concerned
4 as regards
5 regarding

c
1 In terms of / As regards / With regard to / Concerning / Regarding the dimensions, what is the overall size of the module?
2 In terms of / As regards / With regard to / Concerning / Regarding the materials, what is the bodywork made of?
3 In terms of / As regards / With regard to / Concerning / Regarding the schedule, when will the work start?
4 In terms of / As regards / With regard to / Concerning / Regarding the power, what will the maximum output need to be?
5 In terms of / As regards / With regard to / Concerning / Regarding the heat resistance, what sort of temperature will the paint need to withstand?
6 In terms of / As regards / With regard to / Concerning / Regarding the tolerance, what level of precision do you want us to work to?

3a
1 Can be varied considerably
2 Physical but not so extreme that people don't watch graphics
3 Best to try out effects in practice as it's difficult to do in theory

b
1 how much
2 the amount
3 calculate/give a quantity
4 judge/decide
5 measure/test

c
2 the degree to which
3 To what extent
4 to what extent / the degree to which
5 To what extent
6 quantify/determine
7 assess

6a
1 It's being carved from a block of sandstone.
2 He's overseeing the logistics of the project.
3 On a stone plinth
4 How to stop the slings from getting trapped beneath the statue, so they can be withdrawn, after the statue has been lowered onto the plinth by crane

b
drill = cut a hole
horizontal = level
bar = a long piece of metal with a circular section
vertical = at 90 degrees to the ground
lifting eyes = metal rings that hooks can be fixed to for lifting
resin = a type of strong adhesive
a grab = mechanical jaws that grip objects to lift them
friction = resistance to sliding when two surfaces are pressed together

c
1 Drill into the sides of the statue and insert horizontal bars, which could be used for lifting.
2 Drill into the top of the statue and insert vertical bars with lifting eyes, set into the stone with resin.
3 Use a grab on the end of the crane jib, to lift the statue by friction.
1 & 2 are rejected because holes can't be drilled into the statue (even if they were filled afterwards, they would be seen).
3 is rejected because the statue is too heavy and wide.

d

2 couldn't	5 about
3 could	6 another
4 alternatively	7 don't

7b

The stonemasons' suggestion

Use blocks of ice. The blocks would act as temporary spacers between the statue and the plinth, to allow the slings to be withdrawn, and would then melt, allowing the statue to sit down on the plinth.

Potential problem 1: Outdoor temperatures below freezing would prevent the ice from melting. Solution: In this case, blow torches or salt could be used to melt it.

Potential problem 2: Very hot weather would cause the ice to melt quickly. Solution: To compensate for this, larger blocks of ice could simply be used.

8a

Feasibility means the *possibility of doing something*.

9a

1 For the bolts that will be used to fix the beams to the wall
2 Core drilled holes are formed after the concrete walls have been cast, using a diamond drill. Preformed holes are formed by putting plastic tubes into the walls while the concrete is being poured.
3 Space around the bolts, in the holes, to allow their position to be adjusted
4 Positioning the holes precisely or they won't match with the beams
5 Time and cost

b

See audioscript 6.5 on page 91

d

1 The plastic tubes are cheap to buy and quick to put in.
2 It's slow.
3 Within 20mm
4 Within 10mm
5 That they're not positioned accurately
6 The tolerance

e

2 peanuts ☺
3 painstaking ☺
4 perfectly ☺
5 stretching ☺
6 way ☹
7 borderline ☹
8 tall ☺
9 forever ☹
10 leg ☹

e

1 ☺   2 ☺   3 ☺   4 ☺   5 ☺   6 ☹

10

Suggested answers

1 A hammer-action drill would not be suitable for reinforced concrete, as there's no way it could drill through the steel reinforcing bars. Also, the diameter of the holes would be too great to drill using an ordinary drill bit. This is definitely not a feasible solution.
2 This could be a feasible solution. However, depending on the design of the ends of the beams, it might be difficult to get access to the holes after the beams were fitted. It'll be quite a painstaking job, as the beams might cover the holes, making it impossible to get cement into them.
3 This isn't really feasible, as the positions of the holes might be in unsuitable positions on the beams, for example very close to the edges of plates. This would not be acceptable in terms of structural strength. Also, drilling holes through steel beams on site would

be very painstaking and time consuming compared with pre-drilling them during manufacturing.
4 This should be feasible from a structural point of view, but it'll cost an arm and a leg due to the need for additional steel columns. For that reason, it is not a feasible solution.

11

Suggested answers

Better quality materials, for example making a tool from stainless steel instead of mild steel to prevent corrosion.

Lower unit cost, for example using a single-piece component instead of one that needs to be assembled from several parts, to make it faster to produce.

Make life easier for user, for example designing a simpler control panel that's quicker and easier to use, or maintenance-free components such as bearings that don't need lubricating regularly. Examples of other points that could be added: make products function more effectively, make them safer, make them last longer, make them more robust (stronger).

12a

Suggested answers

cables/connections: Improve the user interface by making cables easier to connect and disconnect; reduce environmental impact by making cables only from recyclable materials.

case: Improve aesthetics by offering a range of colours; make manufacturing easier by making the case from a smaller number of components.

ink/toner cartridges: Improve the user interface by making cartridges easier to remove and replace; consumables – make cartridges bigger so they last longer and need to be replaced less often.

paper: Improve reliability by refining mechanisms to help prevent paper blockages; improve output speed by making the paper flow faster.

power: Reduce environmental impact by having the printer switch off automatically when not in use.

software: Improve the user interface by making the software easier to use.

b

Items 2 and 7

c

1 No. The existing design has proved to be effective. The company doesn't have the resources to make fundamental changes to the production process.
2 Once
3 The software has been a major weakness of the existing model.
4 Significantly – it needs to be simpler to use

d

2 invent again
3 improve the details
4 improve overall
5 think again
6 stay (the same)

e

2 ground up
3 room; improvement
4 Achilles heel
5 back; drawing board
6 quantum leap
7 scratch

f

b 4   c 5   d 6   e 2; 7   f 3

g

2 This is the product's Achilles heel.
3 There's no point reinventing the wheel.
4 We started from the ground up with this new design.
5 The new design is a quantum leap.
6 I think there's room for improvement.

13a

The first mechanical mouse was improved by refining its shape: by adding an additional button and a wheel to the top and by revamping the wheel mechanism under the mouse. The mechanism was redesigned to use a ball instead of wheels, although a wheel mechanism was still used inside the mouse; as the ball rolled, it caused the wheels to turn. For the optical mouse, the designers completely rethought the underside of the mouse. Instead of using a ball, they used optical sensors. They also redesigned the connection between the mouse and the computer, making it wireless instead of having a wire. For the touchpad, the designers went back to the drawing board and invented a new system using a sensitive surface.

▓▓ Unit 7

1

Working with machines that have cutting wheels and blades; work at a high level where there's a risk of falling; work in excavations and tunnels where there is a risk of collapse or dangerous gases; lifting heavy objects with cranes where there is a risk of falling objects; processes that use high-pressure vessels and hoses/pipes where there is a risk of explosion; working with high-voltage electrical circuits where there is a risk of electrocution; processes that use flammable liquids and gases where there is a risk of fire or explosion.

2a

Suggested answers

1 hazardous substances: dangerous materials, for example acid, asbestos; PPE: protective clothing and accessories, for example protective gloves, safety glasses
2 harmful: dangerous to health, for example chemicals that cause skin rashes; fumes: vapour or smoke, for example from liquid chemicals that evaporate at room temperature; asphyxiation hazards: danger of suffocation, for example due to concentrations of carbon dioxide / lack of oxygen
3 fire/explosion hazards: substances that could burn or explode if exposed to naked flames or sparks, for example petroleum products, butane/propane gas, alcohol
4 guards: protective shields around dangerous machine parts, for example the guards over the tops of circular saw blades
5 guardrails: rails at waist level to prevent people from falling, for example along the edges of high-level walkways and platforms; emergency exits: doors to allow rapid escape/evacuation, for example fire exits
6 electrical installations: situations involving contact with exposed electrical conductors such as electrical maintenance or work operations close to high-voltage cables
7 noise hazards: loud noise that can damage hearing, for example loud machines

b

a 2   b 7   c 1   d 3

c

2 e	3 b	4 g	5 f	6 a
7 h	8 c		

d

ear protection, gloves, eye protection, mask

e

Suggested answers

1   This is a confined space. You need to test the air using a CO_2 detector.
2   This is a corrosive substance. You need to wear gloves and eye protection, and a mask for protection from the fumes.
3   This makes sparks and is a noise hazard. You need to wear eye protection, ear protection and gloves.
4   This is a harmful substance. You need to wear gloves, and if there's a risk of splashing, eye protection.

3a

Suggested answers

1   An analysis/prediction of the dangers involved in a working operation
2   A safe working procedure/method
3   Some maintenance work, which includes welding, is going to be carried out in the bottoms of some large grain silos (silo = storage tank for solid substances / powders)
4   Getting inside the silos
5   See audioscript 7.2 on page 91

b

1   Risk of someone falling; risk of gas bottles falling on someone
2   CO_2; fumes from metal; dust (explosion hazard)

c

1   Access hazards: external staircase and internal ladder for safe access for workers, lower bottles into silo with a rope and make sure no workers are underneath in silo. Confined space hazards: use a CO_2 detector, use an air extractor.
2   An air extractor could blow dust into the air and make the problem worse.

4

One of the main dangers is from petrol fumes inside the tank, as there's a risk of explosion due to sparks and flames. The workers will have to be careful that there's no petrol inside the tank. The petrol will have to be drained and the inside will need to be washed out with water and detergent. The opening can then be flame-cut through the steel wall of the tank using an oxy-acetylene torch. PPE required for this job is eye protection (a welding mask), gloves and heavy overalls to protect the worker from molten metal. Alternatively, the cutting can be done with an angle-grinder. To be safe, the worker using the grinder will need to wear eye protection, ear protection, gloves and overalls. When welding the new pipe, the welder will need to wear eye protection (a welding mask), gloves and overalls. If arc welding is used and there are other people working nearby or passing by, screens should be placed around the welder to protect other peoples' eyes from flashes. When shot-blasting, the main dangers are to the eyes, and from noise and dust. Screens should be placed around the area and workers should wear eye protection, ear protection, dust masks, gloves and overalls. Before painting, it's important to read the safety documentation provided with the paint, as PPE may be required – for example, gloves, eye protection and possibly masks to protect workers from hazardous fumes. During all the operations, if any work is carried out more than

two metres above the ground, scaffolding should be provided with handrails, as there is a risk of falling (workers should not stand on ladders while working). Also, all workers should wear hardhats.

5a

1   Maintenance work on low-voltage and high-voltage electrical equipment
2   Changing faulty or worn-out electrical parts, such as motors; repairing loose connects or damaged wires

b

Suggested answers

1   A place where a serious danger is present
2   A written form giving permission to work in a restricted area
3   The person responsible for electrical safety for the whole plant, and the only person authorised to issue permits to work
4   The procedure of having a single key to switchboards, ensuring only one person has access to switchgear at any given time

c

1   at all times
2   Under no circumstances should anyone
3   every single time
4   just a single
5   it's vital

d

1	more	3	less
2	more	4	more

e

2   It's crucial/essential/vital to test the circuit is isolated.
3   The alarm should be reset every single time you start the system.
4   It's crucial/essential/vital to check that the cable is not damaged.
5   It's crucial/essential/vital that you should only store non-flammable materials in this zone.
6   Under no circumstances should anyone enter the restricted area without permission.
7   Before pressurising the system, every single connection must be tight.

6c

Suggested answers

1   It's essential that the crew obtain information on weather conditions. It's crucial that pilots are highly trained and experienced. It's vital that a tension release mechanism is in place.
2   Under no circumstances should operatives work on the line without wearing hot suits and eye protection. It's vital that the crew are highly trained.
3   The cables and platform must be checked every single time they are used. It's vital that twin-engine helicopters are used and these must be maintained to the highest standard at all times.

f

Before starting work, it's vital to isolate the circuit at the switchboard. Then, circuits should be systematically tested to be 100% sure that there's no current. During work, it's essential to tighten connections fully. And it's crucial to ensure that no insulation is damaged. To finish, all the wires should be checked – under no circumstances should there be any loose wires. Then the circuit should be systematically tested.

7d

1   Collisions with the line are a hazard, so it's essential to have detailed weather information, especially wind direction and speed. It's essential that the cable has a tension release system in case of snagging.

2   The engineers wear hot suits that channel the electricity and have a fireproof lining to protect against heat.
3   Only twin-engine helicopters are used and they are fully maintained to aviation regulations.

8

Regulations are laws; they are compulsory. For example, if companies breach (break) safety regulations, they can be fined (given financial penalties) and, in serious cases, managers who are responsible for breaches of regulations can be given prison sentences. Standards, such as quality and design standards, are sometimes compulsory, for example the design and manufacture of motorcycle helmets or car tyres. Sometimes, however, they are optional, for example ISO quality assurance.

9a

Suggested answers

Risk of fire/explosion – no smoking, the provision of fire-fighting equipment and training. Danger of people falling from tall structures and into water – handrails required to give edge protection and life jackets need to be worn in certain situations. Risk of skin irritations from petroleum products – gloves and overalls required. Risk of air crashes as helicopters land and take off from platforms – special training required for pilots and special precautions needed for safe operation of helidecks.

b

1   Specific safety regulations
2   Compulsory personal protective equipment; prohibited activities, such as smoking
3   That the obligations are legal requirements

c

2	compulsory	6	legislation
3	prohibited	7	contravene
4	requirements	8	comply with
5	stipulated		

d

2   permitted
3   comply with
4   stipulated
5   contravene
6   legislation; requirements; obligations
7   compulsory

10a

2	stipulated	5	comply with
3	compulsory	6	requirements
4	legislation	7	obligations

b

1   to give the ground crew access to all parts of the helicopter
2   to avoid risk of collisions during takeoff/landing
3   to avoid risk of collisions during takeoff/landing
4   to tie down parked helicopters

12

1   Safety warnings, operating precautions for machines and maintenance instructions on machines
2   Effective notices and instructions are as short as possible, use clear language, and emphasise important points, for example dangers.

13a

a   Could do both
b   Could damage the machine
c   Could injure workers
d   Could damage the machine
e   Could do both

b

1 danger

2 important

14a

1 Because it contains electrical equipment and could cause electrocution

2 A carbon dioxide extinguisher; carbon dioxide gas does not conduct electricity

3 They are for lifting the machine.

4 The machine could be damaged by the lifting force, and if lifted from anchor points that are not secure, could obviously be dropped from a height as a result.

5 Because it could descend, and injure the person cleaning the machine

6 There may be sharp metal off-cuts below the blade which could cut the person cleaning the machine. S/he needs to wear gloves.

b

1 sp: active (*You should do it*)
  wr: passive (*It should be done*)

2 sp: contractions (*shouldn't, it's*)
  wr: word pairs written in full (*should not, it is*)

3 *if* (sp) = *in the event of* (wr); *because* (sp) = *as* (wr); *so* (sp) = *therefore* (wr); *can/could* (sp) = *may* (wr)

15a

Suggested answers

*Objects **should not be placed** in front of the air inlet. The inlet grille **should be kept** free from obstructions, and **should be cleaned** regularly. **In the event of** damage to the inlet grille, the blower **must be stopped** immediately. Serious harm **may be caused** by foreign bodies entering the duct, **as** the unit contains precision-engineered parts revolving at speed, and is **therefore** highly susceptible to damage. **Before** starting the blower, **it is** important to ensure that the external vents at the end of the air-intake duct are open. **When** opening the vents, the adjusting handle **should be** fully **extended. When** closing the vents, the handle **should be** turned **and allowed** to return under the force of the spring. The handle **should not be pushed, as** this **may** strain the spring mechanism, and **therefore** result in damage.*

▓▓▓ Unit 8

1

An automated system can function autonomously, without human control. A manual system requires human control. A Building Management System is a centralised computer system that monitors and controls a wide range of functions in a large building, such as the lights, heating, air-conditioning, smoke detectors, fire alarms, lifts and security systems.

2a

1 It's a very green/environmentally orientated company.

2 Energy saving will be an important consideration in the design.

3 Sensors that detect the presence of people

4 He wants to present two different design options to the client. He describes option one as *a building with maximum automation*.

b

1 ✓   2 ✓   3 ✗   4 ✓

c

2 reading   4 detect; pick up

3 regulate   5 set off; trigger

d

2 control   5 detects; triggers

3 senses   6 set off

4 reading   7 regulate

e

Suggested answers

1 Presence detectors pick up movement and can activate light switches.

2 Smoke detectors sense smoke and trigger fire alarms.

3 Thermostats can regulate room temperature by controlling electric convector heaters.

4 Pressure plates can detect the weight of a person and set off intruder alarms.

3a

1 That the green attitude is shared by all the staff, so they would take care to switch off lights etc. and so there is no need to control everything automatically

2 Instead of automating everything, they would have old-fashioned manual controls.

3 The advantage of operating the lights, etc. manually is that there's no need to supply all the automated controls with electricity. The money saved by not having to buy all the hi-tech gadgets could be spent on planting trees, for example.

4

Suggested answers

A thermostat measures and controls the water temperature in a boiler, and there is also sometimes a pressure sensor for safety. A thermostat measures and controls room temperature in a heating system. A refrigerator also has a thermostat to monitor and control the temperature and a light that is activated by the door opening. Washing machines have thermostats to control the temperature of the water inside the machine. The time of the wash cycle is also controlled. The action of the drum is linked to a safety device that prevents the door from being opened while the drum is spinning.

5a

1 e   2 b   3 a   4 d   5 c

b

1 pressure measurement, for example monitoring the pressure of air inside a compressed air hose

2 temperature measurement, for example measuring the temperature of water in a boiler

3 flow, for example monitoring the amount of fuel flowing along a fuel pipe in an engine

4 level measurement, for example monitoring the level of water in a fuel tank

5 process recorders, for example monitoring the rejected (broken) items in a production process

6a

a A blockage in a pipe causing a build-up of pressure

b A safety valve and a warning system triggered by a pressure differential

c A system for monitoring gas consumption

d Cumulative consumption, the rate of consumption at different points in time, and the frequency of peaks in consumption

e A timescale

f An exothermic reaction

g The temperature of gas at the input point, and at the output point

h The optimum input temperature for the gas

b

2 g   3 a   4 i   5 c   6 d

7 f   8 j   9 b   10 e

c

2 consumption   7 frequency

3 cumulative   8 input

4 rate   9 output

5 timescale   10 optimum

6 cycle

7a

Suggested answers

We need a meter/sensor to measure: the rate of flow of water at the input point; the water temperature at the input point; the rate of flow of gas at the input point; the temperature of the gas burner; the water temperature inside the vessel; the level of water inside the vessel; the steam pressure inside the vessel; the steam temperature inside the vessel; the steam temperature at the output point; the steam pressure at the output point; and rate of flow of steam at the output point.

b

Suggested answers

The cumulative consumption of water and gas; the cumulative output of steam; the peak rates of consumption for water and gas; peak steam output; the frequency of gas use / firing of the burner; the differential between water input temperature and water temperature inside the vessel; the differential between steam pressure inside the vessel and in the output pipe; the differential between steam temperature inside the vessel and in the output pipe.

8a

See audioscript 8.5 on page 92

b

1 temperature

2 light levels

3 day of the week

4 mealtimes

5 commercial breaks on TV

c

1 increase

2 increases; decreases

3 rise

4 rises

5 falls

6 rise; fall

d

1 Because maximum capacity is equivalent to peak demand, there is significant spare capacity during off-peak periods.

2 Being able to generate power during off-peak periods and store it for peak periods

3 Because electrical charge is extremely difficult to store in large amounts.

e

2 g   3 d   4 a   5 b   6 h

7 f   8 e

f

Suggested answer

There is a band of fluctuation between approximately 2,700 and 5,000 Megawatts. Peak demand occurs each day at about 8.00 pm, when there is a very brief blip. The graph shows a trough each night, when demand falls significantly. At the weekend, the range of fluctuation is smaller than it is during the week. Fluctuations in demand are continual – there are no points where demand remains at the same level continuously for a long period of time.

9a

2 peak demand   5 fluctuations

3 continual   6 range

4 blips

b
1 Operating on a start-run-stop-wait basis
2 Momentary blips in demand
3 Frequency of the AC (alternating current) supply
4 A slight drop in frequency indicates that power stations are working at full capacity.
5 Start-up of appliances is delayed slightly by holding the appliance on standby

10a
1 Demand for electricity fluctuates, and power stations need to be able to cope with peak demand (at the top of the range of fluctuation). The problem is that the peak only lasts for a very brief period each day, meaning that power stations have a lot of generating capacity which, most of the time, is not used. Therefore, electric companies try to smooth demand – using spare capacity during demand troughs (at night) to store up energy, which is then used the next day when demand peaks.

11a
1 A senior manager
2 A review of the company's organisation and facilities
3 Optimising efficiency / the use of engineers' skills

b
1 c   2 b   3 a

c
1 A: 50%   B: 50%
2 A: 70%   B: 30%
3 A: 10%   B: 90%

d
2 off the top of my head
3 pretty much
4 nowhere near
5 roughly / somewhere in the region of
6 roughly / somewhere in the region of

12a
1 T
2 T
3 F – they print very few copies

b
1 roughly
2 well over
3 a good
4 the vast majority
5 next to nothing

c
2 Pretty much
3 Nowhere near
4 Roughly / somewhere in the region of
5 Well over
6 Next to nothing
7 Roughly / somewhere in the region of
8 the vast majority

Unit 9

1
Suggested answers
1 Using software to simulate real-life situations. The main advantage of this technique is that testing is often faster and easier to undertake compared with real-life testing. Variables can also be changed easily. The main disadvantage is the lower degree of realism.
2 Testing small models of designs. The main advantage of this approach is that models are quicker and cheaper to build than full-

sized prototypes. The main disadvantage is that their behaviour during tests cannot perfectly simulate that of a full-size prototype.
3 The main advantage of this approach is that tests are totally realistic. The main disadvantage is that full-scale prototypes can be expensive to build and test.

2a
Computational Fluid Dynamics (CFD) is computer software used to assist in aerodynamic design. It models the flow of air over surfaces, such as car bodywork or the fuselage and wings of aircraft. Virtual testing with CFD software is typically done in the early stages of the design process. Wind tunnels equipped with rolling roads allow reduced-scale models of vehicles or full-size vehicles to be tested. Air is blown through the tunnel by powerful fans to create airflows of different velocities which simulate the vehicle travelling at different speeds. The airflow over the surfaces is highlighted with streams of smoke, so that it can be analysed. A rolling road is effectively a conveyor belt which moves beneath the stationary vehicle at the same speed as the airflow, making the wheels turn. This allows engineers to analyse the effects of the spinning wheels on the airflow. Field testing refers to testing in real conditions. For aerodynamic testing of a vehicle, this might involve driving the vehicle at different speeds on a circuit or runway.

b
1 Using a scale model or a full-size mock-up
2 To simulate the turbulence caused by wheels when they're spinning
3 Whether or not the wheels are mostly enclosed by the bodywork
4 They are not a hundred percent reliable; the data needs to be validated by full-scale tests in real conditions.
5 Changeable weather makes it difficult to do back-to-back testing

c
2 mock-up
3 validate
4 acid test; tried-and-tested; trial run
5 back-to-back testing; in the field

d
b tried-and-tested
c in the field
d virtual
e the acid test
f back-to-back testing
g validate
h trial run

e
2 e   4 d   6 a   8 b   10 c

3
First, testing of the parachute could be done using a weight to simulate the mass of the container. The weight should be solid and unbreakable, for example a block of steel, to allow several parachute systems to be tested back-to-back without destroying the container each time. For tests, the weight and parachute could be dropped from a raised platform attached to a crane. Initially, the aim of these tests will be to develop a parachute system that will slow the container's fall as much as possible to minimise the vertical landing speed. Once the parachute system has been developed, and the vertical landing speed has been determined,

tests can then be carried out on the container and deformable structure by simulating this known landing speed. Initially there will be no need to use the parachute, as the container can be allowed to freefall from the crane – the drop height being set so that the vertical landing speed is the same as that reached with a parachute. Initially, reduced-scale, for example half-size, mock-ups could be tested. Then full-scale tests can be carried out. The container design can then be tested with the parachute by dropping it from the crane. This will help to simulate the effects of the wind blowing the parachute and container, thus generating a horizontal (as well as vertical) landing speed. Finally, for the acid test, real life trial runs can be carried out using an aircraft to validate the tests.

4a
Suggested answers
1 Humanitarian aid, for example food and medicine, and military equipment are often airdropped, as they frequently need to be delivered to remote locations with limited transport links.
2 The main advantage is that planes do not need to land and take off again to drop off cargo, saving time and fuel. The main disadvantage is the difficulty of protecting cargo from impact damage.

b
1 decrease – As long as the container remains in the air, its airspeed (its speed relative to the moving air in the atmosphere) will keep decreasing until it has an airspeed of zero – until it is travelling at the same speed and in the same direction as the wind. Therefore, if there is a certain amount of wind, the container will have a degree of groundspeed (horizontal speed relative to the ground), as it moves with the wind. If the aircraft is flying into the wind (in the opposite direction to the wind) when it drops the container, and if the container remains in the air long enough, the container will slow down until it momentarily has a groundspeed of zero. However, if it remains in the air beyond this point, its groundspeed will then begin to increase again in the opposite direction to the aircraft, as it is blown backwards by the wind.
2 higher – The container's vertical speed will keep increasing until, if it remains in the air long enough, it reaches *terminal velocity* – the point at which aerodynamic drag (air resistance) prevents it from travelling any faster.
3 and 4 This will depend on the shape of the container and the distribution of weight within it.

c
They agree on the first two points (horizontal speed decreases and vertical speed increases). They disagree on the last two points (which impact is worse, and what will happen on the ground with a very low-altitude drop).

5a
1 theoretically   4 presumably
2 assuming   5 arguably
3 surely

b
1 Presumably   4 Arguably
2 Assuming   5 Surely
3 Theoretically

c

Agree: Sure; Absolutely; True; Of course
Other phrases: I totally/completely agree
Disagree: I'm not so sure …; I'm not convinced;
Not necessarily
Other phrases: I'm not sure I agree; I disagree;
I totally disagree

d
Suggested answers
1   An aircraft's groundspeed is its speed relative
    to the ground. Its airspeed is the speed it
    passes through the air. Because of the wind,
    the air is usually moving. Therefore, if an
    aircraft is flying into the wind, its airspeed
    will be higher than its groundspeed. If it has
    the wind behind it, its airspeed will be lower
    than its groundspeed.
2   Zero
3   The aircraft would need to fly into the
    wind, and the wind speed would need to be
    very high, higher than the minimum speed
    required for the aircraft to fly.
4   It should fly into the wind so that the wind
    helps the container to slow down.
5   Provided the aircraft flies into the wind,
    higher wind speed will result in the container
    having a lower groundspeed on landing.
    However, above a certain wind speed, the
    container will reach zero groundspeed, then
    start to travel in the opposite direction.
    Beyond this point, even higher wind speeds
    will result in a higher groundspeed in the
    opposite direction.

6b
Suggested answers
1   The container could be flat with a low centre
    of gravity so that it slides along the ground,
    or perhaps spherical with a deformable
    protective structure which allows it to roll
    along the ground.
2   The container could be tall, for example a
    cylinder shape, with a deformable protective
    structure at its base to absorb the vertical
    impact.

7a
Expectations are what you predict, for example
how you think a vehicle prototype will behave
when it's tested in a wind tunnel. Results are
what actually happens, for example how the
prototype actually behaves in the wind tunnel,
based on the completed test.

b
Trial and error means testing ideas to see what
happens. The expression implies that the testing
process is not very scientific, and is simply based
on guesswork.
Unfamiliar territory means an unknown subject,
an area where someone lacks experience.
On a steep learning curve means learning
rapidly, often as a result of being put in an
unfamiliar situation without the necessary
knowledge or experience.

c
See audioscript 9.3 on pages 93 and 94

8a
1   Half full.
2   The opening in the bottle was just slightly
    bigger than the fitting at the end of the
    pump, so there was quite a good seal.
3   Quite powerful, more powerful than expected
4   The bottle tumbled over in the air – it
    wouldn't fly straight.

b
1   thought/predicted
2   didn't expect/predict
3   it was much better than we had hoped

9a
See audioscript 9.4 on page 94

b
They put a plastic beaker, with water inside it,
onto the top of the bottle which made it front-
heavy and increased its inertia.

c
1   according to plan
2   a treat

10b
See audioscript 9.5 on page 94

c
2   practice   5   inadequate
3   more   6   practical
4   less

12
Suggested answers
1   Possible causes: the tyre is inadequately
    inflated or punctured
    Possible effects: the tyre could blow out
    (explode) / the tyre will wear rapidly / become
    damaged.
2   Possible causes: a surge in the power supply,
    too much power being demanded, a short
    circuit
    Possible effect: a circuit breaker being
    triggered, overheating and damage to
    conductors and components
3   Possible cause: there is inadequate paint
    cover to protect the hull
    Possible effect: the hull will degrade rapidly /
    could fail

13a
A mistake with a chicken gun has made clever,
technical people look like fools.

b
1   To fire dead chickens in order to test aircraft
    engines and windshields for their resistance
    to bird strikes
2   Because it was a high-speed train and bird
    strikes were a potential danger
3   The chicken broke through both the
    windshield and the back of the driver's
    compartment.

c
They used a frozen chicken.

d
2   because of; due to; owing to
3   result of
4   because of
5   caused
6   consequently

e
1   because of / due to / owing to
2   caused; consequently
3   because of / due to / owing to; resulted in;
    consequently

14a
See audioscript 9.6 on page 94

1a
Suggested answers
1   They use the kinetic energy, movement of the
    wind, to generate electricity.
2   Advantage: They use a renewable, non-
    polluting energy source that is readily
    available.
    Disadvantages: The wind is not constant, so
    wind turbines cannot function all the time.
    They also have a major visual impact due to
    their height and size, and are relatively noisy.
3   Locations exposed to the wind, such as high
    ground, flat areas and coastal areas

b
Suggested answers
The blades turn due to the air flow generated
by the wind. To function, they need to have
a specially designed aerodynamic profile.
They must also be stiff, to avoid flexing and
consequently hitting the tower, and relatively
light to allow them to turn easily.
The tower must be rigid, to resist the bending
force generated by the pressure of the wind. It
must also have a relatively narrow profile, to
minimise the aerodynamic effect it has on the
blades. When a blade is in the low position,
aligned with the tower, the pressure of the wind
on the blade is reduced, reducing effectiveness,
and causing torsion in the turbine due to
differential pressure on the higher and lower
blades.
The turbine generates electricity from the action
of spinning. To function effectively, it needs to
minimise friction. It must also resist the severe
weather which is common in the areas where
wind turbines are located.

2a
1   The tower
2   Corrosion due to the presence of saltwater
3   Steel and reinforced concrete
4   Because in reinforced-concrete coastal
    defences, the steel reinforcement is often
    exposed, due to erosion, and rusts as a result
5   That just because an installation requires
    regular maintenance, that doesn't necessarily
    mean it's unreliable
6   A comparison of the difference between the
    construction cost of a reinforced concrete
    tower and the cost of repainting a steel tower
    over the period of a concrete tower's lifespan

b
2 e   3 c   4 a   5 f   6 d

c
2   inappropriate   6   inefficient
3   inconsistent   7   unreliable
4   uneconomical   8   insufficient
5   ineffective   9   unsuitable

d
See audioscript 10.1 on page 94

3a
2   suitable   5   inefficient
3   effective   6   insufficient/inadequate
4   inconsistent   7   unreliable

b

Suggested answers

1 Wind turbines are extremely efficient. They use a free, renewable source of energy. They're also extremely reliable, requiring very little maintenance.

2 Clearly, wind turbines need wind to function effectively but wind conditions are inconsistent. For this reason, a wind turbine is a supplementary source of energy. It will still be necessary to have a permanent supply of electricity. However, in suitable locations, wind turbines can work effectively for a significant percentage of time.

3 The most suitable sites are exposed locations. Sites located on the tops of hills, on the windward slopes of hills, near the coast, or on flat, open land are the most suitable.

4 To work effectively, wind turbines should be located away from features that can obstruct the wind, such as buildings or trees. Obstructions can have a negative effect if they are located in front of the turbine, and also if they are relatively close behind it.

4b

See audioscript 10.2 on page 94

c

She doesn't mention centrifugal force.

d

2	bending	7	shear
3	torsion/torque	8	friction
4	expansion	9	contraction
5	pressure	10	centrifugal force
6	tension		

e

2 pressure
3 bending
4 compression; tension
5 shear
6 friction
7 torsion (torque)
8 expansion; contraction

f

Suggested answers

When there is no wind, the columns and legs are all subjected to compression. The legs are also subjected to bending forces. The beam is subjected to a vertical bending force. The insulators are in tension. The foundations are in compression. There are also shear forces between the legs and the foundations.

When the wind is blowing from direction 1, the beam is subjected to a horizontal bending force from the wind. Both columns are also subjected to bending. Legs 1 and 2 are in tension as a result of the wind. Legs 3 and 4 are in compression.

When the wind is blowing from direction 2, both columns and legs are subjected to bending by the wind. Legs 1 and 3 and column 1 are primarily in tension as a result of the wind. Legs 2 and 4, and column 2 are in compression.

5a

Suggested answers

Planes travel much faster than high-speed trains. The fastest high-speed trains can travel at just over 300 km/h. Commercial aircraft flying at an altitude of around 30,000 feet can travel with a groundspeed of around 800 km/h. Therefore, on board trips are typically faster on planes. However, rail networks generally link city centres, which are often more convenient destinations

than out-of-town airports. Planes also tend to be delayed more often than trains, due to air traffic congestion at airports. Large aircraft cannot take off and land immediately after one another due to the need for separation distances for safety, and to allow air turbulence time to clear along the runway after each takeoff and landing. Also, checking in for flights takes longer than boarding trains. For these reasons, overall journey times on high-speed trains can be as short as, or shorter than those on planes over distances of 500 km to 1,500 km.

b

1 Speed, convenience, efficiency and environmental-friendliness
2 To find the best way of transporting people
3 That high-speed electric trains are the most efficient solution

c

1 criterion
2 factor
3 variable

6a

Most TGVs reach 300 km/h. Newer models run at 320 km/h on certain tracks. Most trains are approximately 200 metres long.

b

See audioscript 10.3 on page 94

c

1 It was modified to a certain extent but, with a few exceptions, was essentially an ordinary TGV.
2 100 metres
3 To make it slightly more aerodynamic
4 To reduce the speed of revolution, to limit friction and centrifugal force

d

2 − 50%
3 − 15%
4 + 19%
5 + 68%

e

2	certain	5	marginally
3	significantly	6	substantially
4	slightly more	7	considerable

f

Suggested answers

1 The supply voltage in the catenary cables had to be increased by a considerable amount.
2 To limit oscillation, the tension of the catenary cables was substantially increased.
3 The camber of the track was increased marginally on some curves.
4 The previous record was beaten by a huge margin.
5 In perfect conditions, the TGV could probably have gone slightly faster.

8a

See audioscript 10.4 on page 95

c

1 1,015
2 3
3 20
4 1.2
5 46

e

2 cope with; withstand
3 exceed; surpass
4 intended for
5 able to; capable of
6 incapable of; unable to

f

2	capable	6	unable
3	able	7	incapable
4	withstand	8	exceeded
5	subjected to		

9a

Key information and questions

The supersonic rocket sled ride for tourists is to be located the Australian desert. It is to carry a pilot and two passengers. It must avoid extremes of G force under acceleration and deceleration (max 2 G). Max track length 16 km. Is it feasible to have just 10 km of track? Is that enough safety margin? Is the sled to have steel skids or wheels? Propulsion will be by rocket or jet engine (being looked into by someone else). Braking system − not a water brake, as there is too much G force; possibly a friction system (against rails), an aerodynamic system (flaps or parachutes), reverse engine thrust system or a combination of these.

GLOSSARY

This glossary contains useful technical words from the texts and audioscripts which are *not* covered specifically in the exercises.

Word	Definition	Translation
Unit 1		
bearing	mechanism containing balls or rollers placed around a component which spins, e.g. a shaft, to reduce friction	
belt (drive belt)	closed band placed around two or more wheels (pulleys), allowing one wheel to drive the other(s)	
cable	rope made of many wires, usually metal	
component	individual part of an assembly/mechanism	
electromagnetic	has/uses an electrically generated magnetic field	
foundation	base supporting a building or structure, usually made of concrete	
gears	wheels with cogs (teeth) which mesh together to transfer drive from one wheel to the other where the wheels are side by side	
inertia	the resistance of an object to acceleration or deceleration due to its mass	
lubricant	liquid or viscous solid (e.g. oil) used to reduce friction between moving parts whose surfaces are touching	
(electric) motor	device which transforms electrical energy into rotary motion	
pile	foundation comprising a vertical column of concrete in the ground	
propeller	device with spinning blades used to push boats or aircraft through water or air	
reinforcement	networks of fibres or bars placed inside a material to strengthen it, e.g. steel reinforcement in concrete	
remote control	system used to control a device or vehicle from a distance, usually via a wireless connection	
sheave	alternative term for pulley (see *belt* above)	
solar power	energy from sunlight converted into electrical energy	
strength-to-weight ratio	toughness of a material (ability to resist breaking) relative to its density (density = mass/volume)	
structural engineer	engineer specialising in the design of structures, e.g. bridges	
wind load	force exerted on a structure by the wind	
wireless	signal transmission without a physical connection by wire, e.g. by radio waves or infrared waves	
Unit 2		
aggregate	solid particles or lumps of material used in a mixture, e.g. sand and gravel in concrete	
automotive	related to vehicle design and manufacturing	
blade	cutting device, often metal with a sharp or toothed edge	
cement	lime-based powder mixed with water to make concrete	
chassis	base of a vehicle to which all main components are fixed	
composite (material)	combined materials; consists of a bulk material (called a matrix) reinforced with fibres or bars, e.g. glass-reinforced plastic (plastic matrix with glass fibres)	
conductor	material that conducts (carries) electricity or heat – in engineering, usually refers to an electrical conductor	
electrolysis	passing an electrical current through a liquid or solid in order to separate chemical compounds	
exhaust	system for evacuating smoke or gases, e.g. from an engine	
galvanized	coated with zinc – used to protect steel from corrosion (rusting)	
insulation	protective layer to prevent or reduce conduction of heat or electricity	
ironmongery	collective term for small metal items commonly used in buildings, e.g. door handles, hinges, screws, nails	
kinetic energy	energy in the form of movement, e.g. a spinning wheel	
melt down	change a solid substance into a liquid by heating it	
membrane	thin layer of material, often acting as a barrier, e.g. to prevent water passing	
puncture	hole causing a leak of air or liquid, e.g. in a tyre	
rust	common name for iron oxide – produced when iron corrodes as a result of exposure to air and water	
scrap	used/recovered material intended for recycling; often refers to metal	

Word	Definition	Translation
Unit 3		
acetylene	gas commonly mixed with oxygen in welding (oxy-acetylene)	
ballast	dense material used to add weight, e.g. as a counter-balance or to resist lift	
cable tie	plastic strap used to fix several cables together side by side, or to fix cables to a supporting structure	
casting	pouring molten material into a mould	
earth	electrical connection between a circuit and the ground	
live	in a mains electrical circuit, the wire through which current flows into an appliance – also means a circuit is energised (current is flowing)	
machining	collective term for processes involving cutting, drilling, etc.	
milling machine	machine with cutting wheels used to cut away the surface of metal in thin layers	
neutral	in a mains electrical circuit, the wire though which current flows out of an appliance	
Unit 4		
black bolt	in construction, an ordinary bolt	
cable tray	long metal plate on which cables are laid – designed to support large numbers of cables	
column	vertical support in a structure	
construction joint	joint between two sections of concrete that were poured at different times (where concrete structures are poured in several stages)	
duct	large section pipe, with a circular or square profile, for carrying air; or a protective cover for cables or hoses	
fabrication	making/assembling, often used to describe metalwork	
fixings	collective term for bolts, screws, rivets and clips	
high strength friction grip (HSFG) bolt	bolt which holds plates together by friction (gripping them tightly together) rather than by shear force	
M&E	abbreviation for *mechanical and electrical* – in construction, refers to electrical installations, water pipes, air-conditioning, etc.	
pour (concrete)	place/cast concrete	
slab	large flat area of concrete, for a floor or roof	
Unit 5		
clearance	distance between components designed to fit together closely	
clutch	friction mechanism allowing engine motion to be transferred to wheels progressively	
coolant	liquid in a cooling system	
drag	resistance to movement through a gas or liquid, e.g. when a plane moves through the air	
electrical contact	point where two electrical conductors are connected	
engine	often refers to an *internal combustion engine* – i.e. one which burns petrol or diesel	
fan	spinning device with blades used to generate a flow of air	
filter	material with small holes located in a flow of gas or liquid; used to block solid particles, e.g. to prevent them from damaging a sensitive mechanism such as a pump	
flaps	moveable panels on aircraft wings which increase lift to assist low-speed flight, e.g. during take-off and landing	
fly-by-wire	aircraft controls which operate moveable devices (e.g. flaps) electronically, rather than mechanically	
fuel injection	system for injecting fuel vapour into the piston cylinder of an engine	
temperature gauge	device which shows a temperature reading	
gearbox	case containing shafts with gears, usually with a gearshift mechanism, allowing gears to be moved to change between different gear ratios	
hydraulics	high-pressure oil circuits used to push pistons called hydraulic rams	
isolate	separate an electrical component or part of a circuit from the rest of the circuit – e.g. by opening a switch – to prevent electricity from flowing through it	
landing gear	wheels of an aircraft	
loose connection	electrical connection that is not fully tight, often causing the circuit to be broken, preventing current from flowing	
misfire	when an engine is not running smoothly due to a fuel or ignition problem	
non-serviceable (part)	part that cannot be repaired by maintenance technicians, only by the manufacturer	
piston	mechanism which transfers linear motion (backward and forward movement) to rotary motion (turning movement), usually pushed by expanding gas	

Word	Definition	Translation
radiator	heat-exchange device that dissipates heat into the air, usually from a hot liquid (e.g. coolant) that is pumped through it	
spoilers	moveable panels on aircraft wings which increase drag and reduce lift; used to slow aircraft when descending and on landing	
starter motor	electric motor in an engine used to turn the engine in order to start it running	
suspension	moveable connection between a vehicle's chassis and its wheels, consisting of springs and dampers	
tank	container for storing liquid	
throttle	accelerator control on an engine	
turbine	transforms a flow of fluid (liquid or gas) into rotary movement, e.g. a wind turbine	
valve	mechanism for opening/closing/restricting the flow of gas or liquid along a pipe	

Unit 6

Word	Definition	Translation
beam	long, narrow horizontal component in a structure	
core drill	hole-saw for drilling through thick materials	
crane	machine for lifting heavy objects, able to reach significant heights and distances; includes mobile cranes (which wheel), tower cranes (which are supported by a fixed tower) and gantry cranes (which run along beams)	
dynamic	related to movement, e.g. a dynamic load (= a load generated by a moving object)	
G-force	force of acceleration or deceleration: 1 G is equivalent to the force of acceleration exerted by gravity	
jib	moveable arm of a crane	
lifting eye	ring fixed to a heavy object allowing a hook (e.g. of a crane) to be attached to enable lifting	
low-loader	truck with a low, flat trailer, used for transporting large heavy vehicles, especially construction plant	
slings	flat straps which can be attached to crane hooks and placed under objects in order to lift them	
thrust	pushing force, e.g. generated by expanding gases exiting a rocket	

Unit 7

Word	Definition	Translation
air inlet	point where air enters a device or process – the opposite is air outlet	
arc	electrical current travelling a short distance through the air to flow between two conductors	
blower	pump-like mechanism which generates airflow	
circuit breaker	electrical device which instantly breaks a circuit (switches off the power supply) as a safety measure if a variation in current is detected	
extinguisher (fire extinguisher)	device used for putting out fires; usually a metal container with a hose or nozzle containing water, CO_2, powder or foam	
gas bottle	metal container which contains compressed gas, often in liquefied form	
guardrail	safety rail designed to prevent people falling from high places	
handrail	(as guardrail, above)	
load-bearing	describes a part of a structure or assembly that is designed to resist/transmit force	
moisture-sensitive	can be damaged by water	
off-cuts	waste pieces left over after cutting	
shot-blasting	firing small metal balls propelled by compressed air as an abrasive cleaning process	
silo	large container for storing bulk granular materials such as grain	
strain	change in size/shape of a component (e.g. stretching) due to force	
switchboard	control panel containing several switches for all the individual circuits of an electrical installation	
switchgear	collective term for switching equipment	
transformer	electrical device for modifying current and voltage – a step-up transformer increases voltage and reduces current, a step-down transformer decreases voltage and increases current	

Unit 8

Word	Definition	Translation
AC	Alternating Current	
automation	automatic control of a system, device or process	
CAD	Computer Aided Design – computer software for producing engineering drawings	
conveyor belt	moving belt which transports objects horizontally; often used in manufacturing processes and warehouses	
downstream	further down the direction of flow (e.g. in a river); used in engineering to describe industrial processes and the flow of liquid/air in pipe/duct networks (opposite = upstream)	
electric utility	company which generates electricity at power stations	

Word	Definition	Translation
electrical charge	stored electricity (potential electrical energy)	
exothermic reaction	chemical reaction which produces heat (opposite = endothermic reaction, which absorbs heat)	
flow	movement of a substance, usually a liquid or gas (e.g. along a pipe)	
gizmo	slang term for a technical device, usually electronic – suggests the device is complex	
hydroelectric power	electricity generated using water pressure (hydrostatic pressure)	
mains electricity	domestic electricity supply system	
manual	controlled by a person – the opposite is automatic	
refrigeration	process of cooling to temperatures below atmospheric temperature	
reservoir	man-made lake for storing water, usually for drinking water or hydroelectric power	
standby (on standby)	when a device is ready to operate immediately, e.g. a TV that is ready to switch on when it receives a remote control signal	
vessel	closed tank which can hold a pressure greater than the atmospheric pressure outside it	

Unit 9

Word	Definition	Translation
aerodynamics	study of airflow, e.g. over moving vehicles and aircraft	
aeronautical	related to the design and construction of aircraft	
centre of gravity	theoretical point on the cross-section of an object from which the object's mass is transmitted vertically downwards due to gravity	
compressor	device for pressurising gas (usually air) inside a vessel or network of pipes/hoses	
data gathering	collecting and recording the results of tests for later analysis	
deformable	can change shape	
deploy	release/eject/open, e.g. when skydivers pull the cord of their parachute, the parachute is deployed	
destructible	can be / is designed to be broken/destroyed	
DIY store	*Do It Yourself* store – hardware / home improvements store selling building materials and tools to consumers	
pressure gauge	device which shows a pressure reading, e.g. in bar or psi (pounds per square inch)	
turbulence	disturbed airflow – i.e. air not flowing smoothly around an object	
vacuum	volume containing no gas, e.g. space	
windshield	glass at front of a vehicle or aircraft which the driver or pilot looks through, also called a windscreen in British English	

Unit 10

Word	Definition	Translation
bodywork	the external skin of a vehicle; usually consists of several panels	
camber	angle that is inclined from horizontal, usually at 90 degrees to the direction of travel, e.g. the camber of a road (the slope of the road across its width)	
catenary	downward curved line of a cable when suspended between two supports	
coastal defences	large walls, blocks, etc., constructed to protect the coast from sea/ocean erosion	
corrode	degrade as a result of a chemical reaction, e.g. iron turning to iron oxide (rust) when exposed to water and air	
corrosion	result of material corroding (see above)	
derail	come off the rails, e.g. trains can be derailed	
detonate	trigger an explosion	
fail-safe	cannot fail / go wrong – often used to describe safety systems	
horsepower	historic unit of power, has been replaced by Watts but still used to describe power output from engines	
inaxial	not in a straight line	
opposing forces	forces acting in opposite directions	
oscillation	wave pattern	
reverse thrust	thrust directed in the opposite direction to that which a vehicle/aircraft is travelling in, intended to slow the vehicle/aircraft	
rpm	revolutions per minute, used to measure the speed of rotary motion	
sled	vehicle that slides along (i.e. does not have wheels), e.g. a sled designed to travel over snow	
stress	the force(s) exerted on an object, e.g. tensile stress in a cable that is being pulled in opposite directions	
superstructure	the part of a structure that is above ground level – the opposite is the substructure	

The authors and publishers acknowledge the following sources of copyright material and are grateful for the permissions granted. While every effort has been made, it has not always been possible to identify the sources of all the material used, or to trace all copyright holders. If any omissions are brought to our notice, we will be happy to include the appropriate acknowledgements on reprinting.

Otis for the text and logo on p10, © Otis Elevator Company; DuPont for the material on pp18–19 from the technical guide to Kevlar®, http://www2.dupont.com/Kevlar/en_US/index.html, Copyright © 2008 DuPont; Flow for the text and logo on pp 25–26, courtesy of Flow International Corporation; Nick Spark for the text on p84 adapted from the story of John P Stapp, 'Ejection Site: Fastest Man on Earth', from http://www.ejectionsite.com/stapp.htm

Photo acknowledgements

Alamy Smokeater p31(t), The Photolibrary Wales, p40, Jon Arnold Images p46, Jon Fox p50, Indigo Photo Agency p53(lm), Jesper Jensen p53(rm), Jupiter Images/BrandX p55(b), Martin Shields p55(bm), Patrick Steel p55(tm), Paul Glendell p57, Chris Laurens p78, isifa Image Service s.r.o. p82
Corbis DonHammond/Design Pics p14, Helen King p15, p22, Ron Nickel/Design Pics p26(3), Johnny Buzzerio p30, A.B./A.B./Zefa p31(b), Seth Joel p54, Bettmann p77
DuPont p18
Getty Images Chris Joseph p6, Jeremy Walker p12, Vladimir Rys p16, Erik Isakon p20, Jeffrey Coolidge p26(6), Steve Lewis p26(4), Stockbyte p26(2), The Studio Dog p26(5), Ryan Pierse p38, Jason Edwards p42, Tim Bieber p43, Getty staff p53(l), Louie Psihoyos p56, Lester Lefkowitz p62, Andy Sacks p70, Ed Darack p72
John Ninomiya p29
Peter Amsden/Photographers Direct p53(r)
Science Photo Library Sheil Terry p26(1), Rosenfield Images Ltd p55(t), Edward Kinsman p74

Author acknowledgements

The author would like to thank the following people for their input and support during the project: Nathalie and Aimy Ibbotson for their enduring patience, Jeremy Day for his excellent editorial guidance and unfailing sense of humour, Clare Sheridan for expertly overseeing the project and for her valuable editorial advice, Sara Harden for doing a great job and a great deal of hard work during detailed editing of the proofs, and Nick Robinson for the initial discussions and pointers that helped get the project started and for his invaluable assistance. Thanks also to Kevin Westbrook for his helpful comments on the sample unit. Special thanks to Barry Ibbotson and Greg Allison for allowing me to pick their brains on various technical topics over the Yorkshire puddings.

Designed and produced by eMC Design Ltd, www.emcdesign.org.uk.

Picture research by Alison Prior. Audio production by John Green and Tim Woolf.

Cambridge English for … is a new series of ESP courses for different areas of English for Specific Purposes. Written for professionals by professionals, these short courses combine the best in ELT methodology with real professional practice.

Other titles in the series: